MW01616012

RENAISSANCE

REDEFINING SUCCESS
FOR MODERN MAVERICKS

**MELISSA AARSKAUG
& MICHELE KLINE**

ISBN: 978-1-968061-98-2

Table of Contents

FOREWORD

About the Foreword

We didn't want a foreword from a stranger who's just read our book; we wanted it from the people who've lived it with us. That's why we invited the ones who know us best, our husbands, our moms, and our dads, to speak into these pages. They've seen the unfiltered versions of us: the ambition, the doubt, the pivots, the fire. Their words bring perspective no one else could offer, part love letter, part truth bomb, and set the tone for the radical honesty you'll find in the chapters ahead.

Bryan Hancock, *Melissa's Husband*

If you've ever reached a milestone you thought would bring happiness, only to feel something was missing, you're not alone. Life moves like a river, carrying us toward goals we once thought were ours. We're taught from an early age to follow a "life checklist" – the job, the title, the home, the milestones, as if ticking boxes will somehow unlock contentment. But the truth is, the path we're handed was never designed for the full complexity of our modern lives.

When I met Melissa, she was a driven professional thriving in her career and chasing big opportunities. A globetrotter, a strategic sales leader who thrived in high-stakes conversations and seemed to always be on the move. She had an energy that could light up a room and the confidence of someone who knew how to make things happen. At that time, her life looked like one continuous forward charge.

But over the years, I've watched Melissa step into an entirely new chapter, not by slowing down, but by redefining what forward really means. She has embraced the role of mother to our four children. She has become a caregiver to her parents, a dedicated wife, and a budding entrepreneur building something with heart. I've seen her cross rivers she didn't expect to face, shifting from corporate power moves to late-night feedings, from sales calls to caring for aging parents, from chasing quotas to nurturing dreams.

And through it all, she has embodied a truth I've come to hold close: *Don't wish it were easier, wish you were better. Don't wish for fewer problems, wish for more skills. Don't wish for less challenge, wish for more wisdom.* These words from Jim Rohn could easily be a through-line for her life. She hasn't sought to erase the challenges. She's grown stronger, wiser, and more aligned in the face of them.

Like a river, Melissa has reshaped herself again and again. Not losing her current, but deepening it. She still has the drive and charisma I saw the day we met, but now it's infused with a new kind of power: the courage to define success on her own terms.

This book is the distillation of that journey. It's her invitation for you to step into your own Renaissance. To embrace the seasons of change, to move with both ambition and authenticity, and to let the waters that challenge you also shape you.

The river is moving. The current is calling. Your inner Maverick is ready to lead you to the shore you've been searching for. Step in.

Your Renaissance starts now.

Thomas Aarskaug, *Melissa's Father*

To single out a defining moment in my daughter's life is, in truth, impossible. Her journey has been shaped by countless experiences, each one layering onto the next to build the person she has become and continues to be. What I have witnessed consistently through every chapter, whether in the classroom, on the playing field, in her career, or in her personal life, is an unshakable inner drive. Melissa has always had an instinctive ability to set a goal, give her best effort, and achieve results without needing to announce it or seek recognition. For her, achievement itself has always been the reward.

This discipline, paired with sharp intuition, gave her a remarkable awareness from a young age. She seemed to understand that diligence and persistence would pay long-term dividends, even if the immediate payoff was not visible. That mindset has served her well through the inevitable twists and turns of an indirect, but always purposeful, journey.

Of the long list of moments that shaped her, one that stands out is when she was cut from the softball team in 10th grade. Many would have been discouraged, but Melissa chose a different path. The very next day, she joined the track team. She was not handed a guaranteed spot; instead, she had to compete for her place, earn it, and prove herself. She threw herself into training, refining every detail, shaving fractions of seconds off her times, and steadily building momentum. Through grit and consistency, she began collecting medals and, more importantly, the respect of her teammates and competitors.

The 400-meter became her signature event, and it ultimately carried her to a state championship and even to a national invitational meet. What began as a setback turned into one of the great triumphs of her youth, a testament to her resilience and her refusal to let obstacles define her.

My hope is that readers of this book see in her story a larger lesson: in life, we will all face moments where we can either give up or choose to chart a new route toward excellence. Melissa has always chosen the latter. That tenacity, that personal credo of striving to improve and never settling, is what I believe to be her most enviable quality and one that will resonate with anyone navigating their own path to success.

Becky Aarskaug, *Melissa's Mother*

Anyone reading this book should pause and take to heart the stories and examples within it. They reflect not only what Melissa has accomplished, but also who she is at her core and why she approaches life the way she does. From her earliest days, learning to walk and talk, she showed a constant curiosity about the world around her. She wanted to know how things worked, why they mattered, and who was behind them. That inquisitive nature has never left her and continues to shape the way she learns, leads, and inspires.

Melissa's sense of responsibility and independence showed up early. At just eight years old, she began babysitting for a family down the street with three small children, all under the age of five. Most children that age might shy away from such responsibility, but Melissa embraced it. What seemed like a simple neighborhood job turned out to be an early glimpse of her leadership, patience, and problem-solving abilities.

That family's father happened to be a partner at a civil engineering firm, and years later, he invited her to intern at his firm. During those summers, while her peers were enjoying carefree vacations, Melissa was already immersing herself in the professional world. At the same time, she was working nights and weekends in a restaurant, balancing multiple commitments with determination, all while babysitting. These experiences reinforced the values of hard work, resilience, and the ability to thrive under pressure.

Her drive and willpower have always been constants. Whenever obstacles arose, she found a way not only to overcome them but to use them as stepping stones toward something greater. That combination of curiosity, work ethic, and discipline has been a guiding force in every stage of her journey.

This book, in many ways, is a natural extension of who Melissa has always been. Mentorship has run through her life like a thread, beginning in high school when she tutored her peers and continuing ever since. Whether in professional settings, community efforts, or personal relationships, she has consistently taken the time to guide, encourage, and uplift others.

My hope is that readers see this book as more than just a collection of stories. It is a continuation of Melissa's lifelong commitment to mentoring and sharing lessons learned along the way. If you let it, this book will challenge you, encourage you, and ultimately inspire you to chart your own course with the same curiosity, discipline, and tenacity that define Melissa herself.

Mark Kline, *Michele's Husband*

I'm deeply honored that my beautiful wife asked me to write this foreword for her new book. As her husband, I've had a front-row seat to her journey—from quiet determination to becoming the empowering, influential leader she is today. It's not often I get to share how it all began, but this story is worth telling—because the traits you'll see in these pages are the very ones I've seen her live out, day after day.

I was living in Reno, NV, in 2008 when I first met Michele. Our meeting happened by chance through a mutual friend (thank you, Scott). We first crossed paths poolside—not on a blind date, just two strangers meeting for the first time. At first, Michele struck me as shy and reserved, yet deeply observant and an exceptional listener. Of course, I was drawn to her beauty and her captivating Argentinian accent (which I still admire today), but more than that, I noticed her attention to detail and the thoughtful curiosity behind her questions—qualities that still define her leadership today.

Thirty days later, I reconnected with Michele and invited her to join a group of friends for a night out in Reno. Over the course of the evening, I learned so much more about her—how she grew up in an affluent family in Argentina, studied Communication and Law through sheer determination, and balanced her academic pursuits with her passion for dance, singing, and field hockey. That's when I realized that when Michele set her mind on a goal, she pursued it with relentless commitment and delivered nothing less than excellence.

Across her years immersed in the hospitality world, Michele poured herself into learning every detail of the industry—how it worked, how leaders inspired (or failed to inspire) their teams, and what it truly meant to lead with purpose. She quickly recognized that the most impactful leaders put their team's needs first and lead with both passion and intent. Michele embraced this wholeheartedly, even while balancing the demands of being a single mother to our son Felipe.

One phrase she once shared with me has always stayed in my mind: *"Why not me?"* This mindset became her driving force—whether facing opportunities or obstacles, she believed she had every right to pursue greatness. Even when her confidence wasn't outwardly obvious, her determination was unwavering.

Fast forward to life together—marriage, two more boys, and countless leadership roles. One moment that stands out was when Michele stepped into the role of Chief Operations Officer for a hospitality firm in Miami, Florida. Just one week into her new position, COVID-19 turned the world upside down. For any leader, that would be a trial by fire. Almost immediately, she faced the difficult but necessary decision to reduce staff. Though the task was heavy, she approached it with grace and empathy—making sure each person understood the decision was not a reflection of their worth or performance, but a step required for the survival of the business. Then, going beyond her official responsibilities, Michele personally reached out through her network to connect as many displaced team members as possible with other organizations in need of their talents.

What this taught me was that Michele didn't just take on the role of COO—she took on the personal mission to lead with passion. And this is just one more example of how she's grown into the leader she is today.

The word *influencer* is thrown around often, but real influence isn't about popularity—it's about the impact you leave behind. Those who have experienced Michele's leadership firsthand will tell you it's lasting. True influence is built from personal experience, and more often than not, those experiences are forged in challenge. I like to think of them as *Scars of Perfection*—the marks left behind by moments that tested you but ultimately sharpened your ability to lead.

Michele has collected many such scars over the years, in roles and situations that anyone can relate to. None of us wake up one day with all the answers—it takes time, trial, and failure to gain real wisdom. Michele's gift is her ability to take those scars and shape them into lessons that motivate and inspire. She knows how to strip away the pain from a negative situation and replace it with clarity, purpose, and actionable insight. Through this lens, she helps readers, clients, and followers understand that with the right mindset, any challenge can become a stepping stone toward potential.

She shares this same philosophy in her bestselling book, *360° IMPACT*, where she dives even deeper into the principles of growth, gratitude, purpose, connection, integration, and collaboration. If you haven't read it yet, consider it the perfect companion to the journey you're about to take in this book. Together, the two works offer a powerful blueprint for not just surviving challenges but transforming them into lasting success. *Your own definition of success,* which is what this book is all about!

I'm often approached by people who recognize me simply because they've read something Michele posted, heard her speak, or seen an interview she's given. They describe her as *powerful, enlightening, motivating,* and *lasting.* They talk about how something she said shifted their thinking, gave them the courage to act, or inspired them to push through a challenge.

Michele's ability to blend passion, knowledge, process, and genuine care for people is a testament to her craft. She never misses an opportunity to improve the way we live, work, and lead. More importantly, she leaves a mark—not just on the moment, but on the mindset of everyone she touches.

As her husband, I am grateful for the chance to write this foreword—not only because I get to honor her journey, but because I know the value of what's inside this book. Michele doesn't just talk about leadership—she lives it. She doesn't just speak about purpose—she embodies it.

And now, it's your turn. As you read, I encourage you to lean in—not just to the stories, but to the lessons behind them. This book can create real change in your life if you allow it to. Let Michele's experiences challenge the way you think, push you to raise your own standards, and remind you that every setback holds the seed of possibility.

Because if there's one thing her journey proves, it's this: the question isn't, "*Why me?*" It's, "*Why not me?*" And the next bold step is yours to take.

Jorge Castex, *Michele's Father*

When Michele asked me to answer the question—*"What's one defining moment when you knew I was going to live life on my own terms—and how did it make you feel as my father?"*—my mind immediately went back to a fall when she was about eleven years old.

At the time, our church was sponsoring a school in great need. They didn't have the basics for winter—coats, boots, and gloves. I figured Michele would be concerned, maybe want to donate a piece of clothing or two. But she didn't just care—she mobilized.

She gathered a group of her friends from the neighborhood, sat them down, and made them commit to a mission: every weekend, for three months straight, they would ride their bicycles through the streets, knock on doors, and collect winter gear for kids they had never met. It didn't matter if it was raining or if the donations were small—every weekend, without fail, they were out there.

I remember watching her map out routes with her friends, load up bags until they were almost too heavy to carry, and keep track of every single item they collected. There was no adult telling her what to do, no reward at the end—just her own conviction that this was necessary, and she was going to see it through.

That winter, I realized two things. First, my daughter didn't need anyone's permission to do the right thing. And second, she wasn't going to live life quietly. She was going to follow her own compass, no matter how unconventional the path. As a father, it made me proud beyond words—but I also knew it meant her life would be full of challenges most people avoid.

What I didn't know then was how much that eleven-year-old girl's spirit would grow into the woman who co-wrote this book. The same fire that kept her pedaling through rainy streets is here in these pages. Michele has always been willing to put in the work, to lead from the front, and to bring people with her toward something better.

For every woman reading this, I hope you take this lesson from my daughter: you are never too young—or too busy, or too small—to decide that you're going to make a difference. And once you decide, don't let go.

Silvia Castex, *Michele's Mother*

For as long as I can remember, Michele has been fiercely determined. If she set her sights on something—whether it was a childhood dream, a career milestone, or a deeply personal goal—there was no halfway effort. She would work, fight, adapt, and persist until it was achieved. Giving up was never an option.

But her perseverance has never been about her alone. Just as strong as her drive to reach her own goals has been her instinct to protect and defend others. I've watched her step in for people who couldn't speak for themselves, fight battles that weren't hers to fight, and stand up for what's right even when it came at a personal cost. She's never been afraid to face conflict if it meant protecting someone or holding the line on her values.

Those two traits—relentless perseverance and fearless advocacy—are woven into every part of who she is, and they are at the heart of this book. I've seen how they've carried her through the highs and lows of her life, and I know they will resonate with every woman holding these pages.

This isn't just another book about success. It's an invitation to redefine it on your own terms, to honor the parts of yourself that the world may have asked you to dim. Michele lives what she teaches here—and if you let her words sink in, you'll start to see the places in your own life where you can stand taller, speak louder, and pursue what matters to you without apology.

Reading this, you'll get a glimpse of the woman I've known all her life—the one who refuses to let obstacles define her and who will never stop believing in the power of standing up for yourself and others. My hope is that her stories and insights will not only inspire you, but also remind you that your own determination and courage are closer to the surface than you think.

A NOTE FROM YOUR FELLOW MAVERICKS, MELISSA & MICHELE

Welcome, kindred spirit.

Before you dive into these pages, we wanted to share a little piece of our hearts and the story of how *Renaissance* came to be.

We (Melissa and Michele) first crossed paths over sixteen years ago, and from that initial meeting, it felt as though we'd known each other for a lifetime. Two souls cut from the same cloth, ambitious, driven, yet always sensing there was something *more* than the prescribed definitions of success we were handed.

Though our individual journeys to this moment couldn't have been more different, one paved with bold, sometimes terrifying, leaps of faith and reinvention, the other a testament to hard-won resilience, the power of community, and steady, determined growth, we both arrived at the same profound realization: success without soul, achievement without alignment, simply isn't success at all. We'd both navigated the fear, taken the risks, and grown immensely through the discomfort of breaking our own molds.

That shared understanding, those hard-earned lessons, became the bedrock of *Renaissance*. We looked around and saw so many incredible women, just like you, wrestling with the same feelings of burnout, misalignment, and the quiet hunger for a life that felt truly their own. We knew we had to create a space and a guide to help others push that reset button, to challenge the external pressures, and to boldly chart a course toward a future that felt not just successful, but deeply fulfilling and authentically *theirs*.

This book is born from our belief that you absolutely can have it all, once you redefine what "all" means to *you*. It's infused with our experiences, our own transformations, and practical tools like the 7 Renaissance Woman Archetypes, designed to help you unlock your unique Maverick power.

Our deepest wish is that as you read, you feel seen, understood, and fiercely empowered. We hope you discover the courage to shed what no longer fits, embrace your own unique way of leading and living, and step into the most vibrant, unapologetic version of yourself.

This is more than a book to us; it's a movement. And we're honored to be on this journey with you.

With Maverick spirit,
Melissa & Michele

INTRODUCTION

---

*"I am not free while any woman is unfree,
even when her shackles are very different
from my own."* —Audre Lorde

Welcome to the Renaissance.

You've spent your life checking boxes, hitting milestones, and striving to match a definition of success that never quite felt like your own. Maybe it got you far, but not full. Maybe it earned applause, but it never quite gave you peace. If you're honest, maybe you've done everything "right"… and still felt wrong inside. You've worn the heels, carried the pressure, smiled through meetings, and silenced your gut to stay likable, strategic, and professional. You've built résumés, teams, and lives that look admirable, but feel off.

You are not alone.

According to McKinsey's Women in the Workplace report (2023), 43% of women leaders are burned out, compared to just 31% of men. And it's not just stress; it's misalignment. Over 75% of women say they've felt the need to downplay their authenticity at work to fit in, be taken seriously, or avoid being labeled "too emotional," "too ambitious," or "too much." Let that sink in: three out of four women are hiding in plain sight.

But not you. Not anymore. Because something inside you is stirring, not just dissatisfaction, but a deep knowing. A hunger. A pull toward truth that can no longer be ignored.

She doesn't arrive with fanfare. She doesn't wait for a title. The Renaissance Woman is forged in the friction between who she was told to be and who she knows she's meant to become. She's bold, but not always loud. Ambitious, but not always conventional. She may have taken detours, paused for others, or rebuilt herself from scratch, but she never stopped becoming.

You know her because you are her. You've felt the whisper: *There's more than this.* You've tried the formula, followed the rules, succeeded in ways that looked good, but didn't feel true.

And now? You're ready for a new definition of success. One that actually fits. One that sets you free. One that you get to author, not inherit.

This book is your invitation **and your guide** to remember who you are beneath the performance. To strip away the expectations and step into something more real: your Renaissance. A reawakening of identity, purpose, and unapologetic power.

We don't offer simple formulas; we offer a framework built on truth. Real stories. Raw lessons. **And practical pathways** that don't just ask you to think, but to return to yourself, **equipped and empowered**. Because redefining success doesn't start with a strategy; it starts with a decision to become the most honest version of you.

You'll hear from both of us, Melissa and Michele, two women who, in different cities and different seasons, came to the same realization: success without self is not success at all.

This book is structured as a two-part journey.

In Part I, "The Awakening," we'll walk with you through the essential shifts required to redefine success on your own terms. Every chapter cracks open a part of that journey. The unraveling. The rebuilding. The rising. We'll explore how to break through fear, cultivate resilience, take aligned risks, anchor into your identity, build authentic community, and truly embody the spirit of a modern Maverick.

Then, in Part II, "Embodying Your Inner Maverick," we'll dive deep into the 7 Renaissance Woman Archetypes. This is where your personal transformation becomes even more focused. You'll discover your dominant archetype(s) and gain tailored strategies to leverage your unique strengths and navigate your specific challenges. This isn't about boxing you in; it's about unlocking the most potent and natural ways for you to lead and live.

This book doesn't ask you to become someone new. It asks you to come home to yourself. And with each story, **each insight, and each archetype explored,** you'll be invited back to your center through truth, reflection, **actionable steps,** and radical self-trust.

This is your permission to begin again, with intention. To rewrite the story. To reclaim your power. To redefine what it means to rise.

This is not just a conversation. It's a reckoning. It's a revolution. It's a return. This is your Renaissance. Let's begin.

PART I

THE AWAKENING – UNDERSTANDING THE RENAISSANCE WITHIN

CHAPTER 1

The Rise of the Modern Maverick

*"I never dreamed about success.
I worked for it."* —Estée Lauder

We live in a world that loves to hand women scripts. Be polished. Be powerful. Be perfect. Be quiet. We're praised for fitting in even when we're dying to break out. You may have found yourself, as we did, becoming a "professional chameleon" adept at showing up, solving problems, staying late, and being the one who outwardly "has it all together". We were just doing what high achievers do. But one of the things we both have in common is that we didn't always know we were performing. That is, until we weren't. And when we finally stepped off that performance treadmill, the crucial question emerged: If I'm not chasing validation... who am I?

The Outdated Playbook of Success

Success. A word that often carries the weight of an elephant. From a young age, many of us are handed an outdated playbook, told what success *should* look like climbing the corporate ladder, achieving financial milestones, balancing work and life seamlessly (a feat often feeling like fiction), and always, relentlessly, striving for more. Being executive women, many of us have mastered this game. We checked the boxes, earned the titles, led the teams, and built the legacies. But at what cost?

The truth is, this conventional playbook was never designed with the full spectrum of women's lives and aspirations in mind. It was built with a singular vision of success, one that rarely accounted for the complexities we navigate. Despite women making up nearly half the workforce, we still hold only a fraction of leadership roles, with just 10.4% of Fortune 500 CEOs being women. For those who do reach the top, the journey is often far more grueling than for their male counterparts.

Our responsibilities also extend far beyond the boardroom. The double burden of leadership and life management is a stark reality. Even in dual-career households, women spend an average of 4.5 more hours per week on unpaid domestic labor than men. Success, as it has been traditionally defined, demands not just professional excellence but also an unspoken expectation to manage everything else (family, home, and emotional labor), without missing a beat. Is it any wonder that a 2023 McKinsey report found that 43% of women leaders are burned out, compared to 31% of men? We are often overworked, overcommitted, and still feel the need to be overqualified just to be seen as competent. The pressure to be competent without being threatening, powerful yet palatable, is a burden few men ever have to consider. The weight of these unspoken rules makes the conventional idea of success not just exhausting, but often impossible to sustain.

Why the Old Rules No Longer Work

Let's be honest, the traditional version of success has been lying to us for years. It shows up in a sleek suit, clutching a six-figure paycheck, driving a luxury car, and sipping an overpriced latte, whispering that happiness is just one more promotion, one bigger house, or one harder hustle away.

But here's the plot twist: That version of success? For many, it's a scam. For decades, we have been sold a definition that demands we sacrifice sleep, sanity, family time, and sometimes even our souls.

If this sounds familiar, if you've felt the deep misalignment between the life you've built and the one your soul craves, you're in the right place. This isn't about dramatically quitting your job, moving to a remote island, and making artisanal candles (unless that's genuinely your calling, in which case, go for it!). It's about breaking free from the toxic idea that success is a rigid, one-size-fits-all formula dictated by everyone except *you*.

Discovering the Modern Maverick Woman

So, what does it mean to be a Maverick woman in today's world?

She is the "Renaissance Woman" we spoke of in the introduction, forged in the friction between who she was told to be and who she knows she's meant to become. She's bold, but not always loud; ambitious, but not always conventional. She understands that success is not a static prize but is seasonal, evolving, and deeply personal. She knows that sometimes the most powerful move isn't climbing higher, it's stepping sideways into alignment.

Being a Modern Maverick means:

- **Questioning the Script:** She challenges the scripts she's been handed about what success, leadership, and womanhood "should" look like.
- **Authoring Your Own Definition:** She's ready to shed labels, limitations, and "shoulds" to reclaim her own definition of success, one that resonates with her core values and brings fulfillment, not just accolades.
- **Embracing Authenticity:** She stops performing and starts remembering who she truly is beneath the titles and expectations.
- **Valuing Evolution:** She recognizes that true success isn't about holding on, but about knowing

when to let go, pivot, and evolve. Her journey
might involve detours, pauses, or rebuilding from
scratch, but she never stops becoming.

This book is an invitation to awaken that Modern
Maverick within you. We, Melissa and Michele, have lived
this. We've been where you are, felt the pressure to perform
and conform, and ultimately broke free to redefine success
on our own terms. And we know this: you already have
everything you need to create the life you actually want. All
you have to do is unlearn and reinvent.

In the next chapter, we'll explore how to start redefining
success from the inside out, challenging those external
measures and truly uncovering what fulfills you. We'll
share our personal stories of breakdown and breakthrough
in detail, showing how we shed our own labels and
"shoulds" to forge paths that felt true. For now, let's reflect
on the playbooks we've been given and begin to question
who wrote them.

Key Takeaways for the Modern Maverick:

- The traditional playbook for success is often
  outdated and wasn't designed for the complexities
  of women's lives.
- Chasing external validation and conventional
  milestones can lead to burnout and misalignment
  rather than true fulfillment.

- A Modern Maverick questions societal scripts and is willing to define success on her own terms, valuing authenticity and evolution.
- Real success begins when you stop performing and start living in alignment with who you truly are.

Reflective Questions:

What parts of the "traditional success playbook" have you been following, and how have they served (or not served) you?

_____

_____

_____

_____

In what areas of your life do you feel you are "performing" rather than living authentically?

_____

_____

_____

_____

What does the term "Maverick woman" stir in you? What aspects of it resonate with your own experiences or aspirations?

_____

_____

_____

_____

CHAPTER 2

Redefining Success from the Inside Out

In the last chapter, we explored the outdated playbook of success and introduced the Modern Maverick, the woman ready to question those scripts and author her own path. Now, we delve into the heart of that authorship: the personal, often messy, but ultimately liberating journey of redefining success from within. This means challenging the external measures we've been handed, uncovering what truly fulfills *you*, and beginning to craft a life that reflects your authentic values, not just a polished résumé.

But how do we begin when we're juggling so much?

No Time Is Ever Perfect, So Why Wait?

Despite carrying the burdens of an outdated success model, we often wait for the "perfect" moment to take action, whether it's applying for a leadership role, launching a business, making a career pivot, or finally prioritizing our own needs. But here's the truth: there is no perfect time.

For women, especially executive women, life is an ongoing balancing act. We are managing multiple roles, leading teams at work while simultaneously being caregivers, decision-makers, and emotional anchors at home. Whether it's navigating sandwich parenting (caring for both young children and aging parents), helping kids transition to college, choosing the right schools, or making financial and life-changing decisions, the weight of responsibility never eases.

And yet, despite these demands, women are often conditioned to wait until everything aligns before making bold moves. We see this in data: women apply for jobs only when they meet 100% of the qualifications, whereas men apply when they meet just 60% (Harvard Business Review). This perfectionist mindset isn't just internal; it's reinforced by a system that scrutinizes us more, expects us to prove ourselves at every step, and punishes us for perceived risks.

Even when we do push forward, the reality of unpaid labor at home remains. Women in dual-career households still spend an average of 10 additional full-time workweeks per year on unpaid labor compared to men (OECD). When do we get the "perfect" moment to prioritize our own success amidst this? The longer we wait, the more time we lose. We are overextended, overworked, and still trying to check every box before we allow ourselves to step into new opportunities. But waiting until conditions are ideal only delays the life and success we deserve.

Actionable Step:
Move Forward Now, Not Later

Identify one area in your life where you've been holding back, whether it's pursuing a new role, advocating for yourself, or making a major life change. Instead of waiting for the "right time," take a small, tangible step forward today. Maybe it's updating your résumé, scheduling a networking conversation, signing up for that course, or simply deciding that you are ready now. The perfect time will never come. Progress starts the moment you do.

This commitment to moving forward, in the face of imperfection, is the first step in crafting a new narrative. As we, Melissa and Michele, discovered in our own lives, redefining success often begins when an old dream unravels or a prescribed path leads to an unexpected dead end. It's in those moments of pivot that the most authentic definitions emerge.

Melissa's Story -
From Setback to Breakthrough

At 14, I was all in on softball. I wasn't just playing, I was excelling. A freshman balancing travel ball, a state championship team, and my high school squad, I lived and breathed the game. It was more than a sport; it was part of my identity.

Then, in my sophomore year, everything changed.

During tryouts, I was coaching another player on how to catch a fly ball when my coach, misreading my signal, launched a pop fly toward me. Before I could react, the ball struck me in the face, leaving me with a concussion and an abrupt end to my tryout. When the final roster came out, my name wasn't on it. I had been cut.

The devastation wasn't just about losing a spot on the team; it was about losing a dream. I had worked, sacrificed, and given everything to this sport, and suddenly, it was gone. What do you do when something you love is taken from you, not because you weren't good enough, but because life threw an unexpected obstacle in your way? For a while, the loss stung. I grieved the end of my softball career. I replayed every moment, every sacrifice I had made for a sport that no longer had a place for me. I wasn't just mourning a game; I was mourning a part of myself.

And then, something unexpected happened.

The Pivot That Changed Everything

The next day, the track coach approached me with an offer: "Come run with us." I wasn't a runner. I had never trained for track, never competed on a relay team. I didn't understand why anyone ran for fun. To me, running was punishment, the thing you did when you made a mistake in a game, the grueling sprints at the end of practice that left your legs burning. It wasn't something I had ever considered pursuing. But with nothing to lose, I said yes and showed up to tryouts. I wasn't the fastest. I wasn't the strongest. But I kept up. I worked hard. I pushed myself in ways I never had before. By the end of the season, I was standing on the podium at the state championships, finishing second in the relay.

But it all could have gone another way. I could have told the track coach no. I could have stayed in my comfort zone, avoided the risk of failing, and let the opportunity pass me by. It would have been easier. Safer. But what if saying yes led to something unexpected? What if stepping into the unknown wasn't about proving anything to anyone but about proving to myself that I was capable of more than I realized? I had two choices: stay where I was or carpe diem and see what was on the other side. I chose the latter. I took the opportunity, laced up my shoes, and ran, not just on the track but toward a version of myself that wasn't afraid to take a leap.

Reinvention Takes Work

I didn't get to state easily. It wasn't as simple as showing up to practice and suddenly excelling. The transition from one sport to another didn't happen overnight. I trained relentlessly, spending weekends working out with my dad and brother, both of whom pushed me beyond my limits. My brother was faster, and chasing him literally forced me to sharpen my speed. My times got better, but track wasn't just about physical endurance; it was a mental game, too. I had to shift my mindset, change my focus, and even adjust my diet. If I was going to commit to this, I had to be all in. And I was.

But committing to something new didn't erase the heartbreak of what I had lost. Letting go of softball wasn't just about leaving behind a sport; it was about leaving behind the identity I had built around it. But what seemed like a career-ending failure in one sport turned into a championship-level success in another.

Track didn't just give me a new sport, it gave me a new purpose. I wasn't just running races; I was building resilience. I wasn't just competing; I was leading.

Over time, I became the captain of the team, guiding and motivating my teammates the same way I had once done in softball. Track pushed me to develop discipline, mental toughness, and the ability to rally a team toward a shared goal. Leadership wasn't just about personal performance; it was about inspiring others to rise to their potential. And the success didn't stop there. I continued to win many more medals, proving to myself that I was more than just a softball player; I was an athlete, a competitor, and a leader, no matter the arena. Leadership wasn't about the spotlight. It was about helping others rise, too.

The Lesson? Success Requires Evolution

My story mirrors the pivots we all face in our careers and lives. We rise, we master, we win, until one day, the rules change. The industry shifts. The role disappears. The goals no longer inspire us. Many of us have built entire careers in one lane, only to realize that lane no longer serves us. Maybe we've hit a plateau, lost passion, or feel the urge to redefine what's next.

But the truth is that success is never singular. And reinvention is not a setback; it's an evolution.

Like me, when one door closes, the strongest leaders don't sit in the loss. They step into the next challenge, even when it's unfamiliar. Because real success isn't just about achieving goals, it's about having the courage to rewrite them.

Michele's Story - A Voice Silenced; A New Path Found

Meanwhile, on the other side of the globe, music was my world at 14. I attended an all-girls private British school in Argentina, where I was part of an internationally recognized choir.

Singing was everything to me. The thrill of performing, the harmonies blending, the power of music to move an audience, it was the one thing that made me feel truly alive.

And I wanted more. There was a prestigious private music academy called Pianissimo, the kind of place that could elevate my skills, refine my voice, and maybe, just maybe, launch me into a career in music. And let's be honest, everyone who was serious about singing was doing it. If you weren't at Pianissimo, you weren't even trying. Sounds dramatic, I know. The classes were after school, perfectly fitting into my schedule, and despite the steep tuition, my parents found a way to say yes. I was ecstatic. This was my moment.

Then came the audition. I gave it everything I had. But instead of a straightforward acceptance, I got a condition, literally. "We'd love to work with you, but before we can accept you into the program, you need to get checked for vocal cord nodules." Not exactly the answer I was hoping for. Vocal cord nodules?! It sounded terrifying, like something that would end up on a medical drama with a surgeon dramatically announcing, "We need to operate... on the voice!" I soon learned they were noncancerous growths, like calluses, caused by the overuse of my voice. Basically, my vocal cords could develop blisters from too much ambition. They could make my voice sound hoarse, breathy, even painful. The treatment? Surgery. Rest. Speech therapy. No guarantees, kind of like spending a fortune on music lessons and still ending up singing in the shower.

My world crumbled. Everything I had envisioned, performing at an elite level, training at Pianissimo, taking my singing to the next stage, was suddenly uncertain. I felt like I had been running at full speed toward my dream, only to crash headfirst into an invisible wall. OUCH!

What now? Quit singing? Give up?

A New Stage, A New Beat

I refused. I continued performing in my school choir, singing at prestigious establishments, embracing every note, even with the weight of my diagnosis hanging over me. But I also had to pivot. The rigorous training Pianissimo required wasn't an option while undergoing treatment. With everything else in my life, school, the high academic expectations, the pressure to excel—I had to make a choice.

So, I channeled my energy into another love: dance. But this wasn't something entirely new to me—I had been dancing since I was six years old. Dance had always been a part of my life, something that brought me joy and balance alongside my passion for music. Celtic dance, jazz, tap—I threw myself into movement the way I had once thrown myself into song. And you know what? It was just as exhilarating, just as fulfilling.

I wasn't abandoning my love for singing, but I was redefining what success looked like for me. It didn't have to be, "Pianissimo or nothing". My renaissance wasn't about holding on to one single path—it was about embracing new possibilities. I danced all through my university days, performing whenever I could, letting it become a central part of my identity.

Letting Go and Letting Dreams Grow

Even now, I still dance when I get the chance. It's a part of me, a reminder that success doesn't have to be rigid—it can evolve, just like we do.

That experience shaped me. It taught me that success isn't about clinging to one rigid dream—it's about allowing yourself the flexibility to evolve, to pivot, to *create new definitions of success when life forces you to rewrite the script.*

I still sing in the shower like I'm headlining a sold-out stadium (with shampoo bottles as my adoring fans), in the car—where stoplight spectators give me that "Is she okay?" look—and during the occasional Disney musical with my kids, who now treat my performances like a family inside joke. They roll their eyes, but I know deep down, they're impressed. Let's be real—no one, and I mean no one, delivers "A Spoonful of Sugar" quite like I do. (Okay, maybe Julie Andrews, but she had a whole orchestra. I make do with a kitchen spatula as a mic.)

A New Definition of Success: Yours to Author

Melissa's story of an unexpected injury leading to a new athletic passion, and Michele's journey from a potential singing career cut short to embracing dance, highlight a crucial truth: the path to a fulfilling life often involves redefining success on our own terms, especially when external validation or a preconceived notion of achievement is stripped away. Both stories show a pivot, a moment of loss that, when met with courage and openness, transformed into an opportunity for authentic growth and a new, more personal definition of success.

So perhaps it's time to rewrite the script entirely. The old model of success told us to work harder, climb higher, and chase titles at any cost. But the new model recognizes that true success is not about endurance, it's about intention. It's about defining success on our terms, prioritizing sustainability over exhaustion, and creating a life, not just a career. It is about knowing that power isn't just in holding on, but in choosing when to let go, pivot, and evolve. This is not failure. This is the rebirth of success, one that is personal, sustainable, and deeply fulfilling.

Spoiler alert: You already have everything you need to create the life you actually want. All you have to do is unlearn and reinvent! We know this because we have lived it. We have both found ourselves (at one point or another) trapped in society's definition of success, feeling stuck on paths that were not truly our own. We broke free, and now, we want to help you do the same.

Success is not just about reaching a destination; it is about how we feel during the journey. It is about waking up excited, feeling aligned with our choices, and having the freedom to shape our lives in a way that fuels us rather than depletes us. And trust us, it is a game-changer when you stop chasing someone else's definition of success and start writing your own rules.

But what happens when the dream you are chasing suddenly disappears? What do you do when everything you worked for gets ripped away in an instant? As Melissa and Michele's experiences show, you find a new way. You unearth a different strength. You begin again.

Key Takeaways for Redefining Success:

- True fulfillment often lies beyond external measures of success; it's found in aligning with your authentic self.
- Setbacks and unexpected obstacles can be powerful catalysts for re-evaluating your path and discovering new passions.
- Redefining success is an active process of letting go, pivoting, and having the courage to author your own rules and definitions.
- Progress begins the moment you decide to move forward, even if the timing doesn't feel "perfect."

Reflective Questions:

What definition of success did you inherit and is it still serving you?

_____

_____

_____

Describe a time you had to pivot or redefine success for yourself. What did you learn from that experience?

_____

_____

_____

_____

_____

If fear and external validation were not factors, what would your ideal vision of success look like for this season of your life?

_____

_____

_____

_____

_____

What is one small, tangible step you can take *today* to move closer to a life that reflects your authentic values?

_____

_____

_____

_____

CHAPTER 3

Resilience in Action

"I can be changed by what happens to me.
But I refuse to be reduced by it."
—Maya Angelou

Resilience. It's a word often associated with stoically pushing through until you break. But that's not the resilience we're talking about. True resilience isn't about silent endurance; it's about knowing when to adjust, when to rest, and ultimately, when and how to rise. The narrative we've often been given, especially as women, is that strength means silence, that leadership is stoicism, that grit must be glorified, and that struggle is definitive proof of our worth. But this definition of resilience isn't just outdated, it's dangerous.

According to Lean In's Women in the Workplace Report, 42% of women say they are burned out. Not tired. Not stressed. Burned out. And yet, nearly 60% say they continue to show up, overextend, and remain silent, often out of fear of being seen as weak, unreliable, or replaceable. This highlights how the old model of "resilience" can be harmful.

Here's the truth we want to explore: Resilience isn't about hiding the mess. It's about showing up *with it*. It's not some badge you earn only after you've perfectly bounced back; it's a conscious decision you make while you're still in the fall, a testament to your power even in the midst of struggle. It's about learning from everything, not just enduring everything. This form of resilience is indeed gritty, often messy, and profoundly powerful. And sometimes, the most powerful forms of resilience aren't visibly dramatic. Sometimes resilience sounds like a quiet "No." Sometimes it looks like strategically stepping away. Sometimes it feels like choosing peace over the illusion of perfection. In a world that praises relentless hustle and often shames the need for pause, choosing to realign is a revolutionary act of true strength. It's a muscle you strengthen by showing up for yourself, even and especially, in the mess.

Melissa's Story - Lead with the Leap: Resilience in Forging a Path

When I decided to move to a different city for college, my brain told me to stay in Las Vegas, just like so many of my high school peers. But my gut told me to leave, to start fresh, to build something new for myself. I knew it would be different, hard, and scary. But I decided to look at it as an adventure. What's the worst that could happen? I told myself. I'll go for a year. If I don't like it, I can always come back. I just had to make it through the year.

My mom was the one who drove with me from Las Vegas to Reno for my first year at the University of Nevada, Reno. An eight-hour trip, just the two of us. By the time we arrived, I was a mix of excitement and nerves, realizing that this was it, I was stepping into the unknown, with no safety net, no familiarity, and no idea what was ahead. I'll never forget walking into my dorm room for the first time. My roommate was from Alaska, a vibrant, friendly redhead who instantly made me feel welcome. It was my first time ever sharing a room, and I quickly realized it was going to be an adjustment. She had late-night music rehearsals; I had early morning engineering classes and sports training. Our sleep schedules clashed, our routines were different, but we learned to adapt. Within a month, we found our rhythm and became good friends.

Our dorm wing housed eight women, with four rooms connected by a shared living space. It was a lively environment, sometimes too lively. Meanwhile, I had to wake up before dawn for classes and workouts. At first, I struggled to balance my need for rest and focus with the constant activity around me. But I quickly realized that if I didn't speak up for myself, no one else would. I had to find my voice, set boundaries, and advocate for what I needed. It was uncomfortable at first, but I learned to ask for what I needed while still being part of the community. That was my first real lesson in resilience, not just enduring, but actively adapting and leading from my own truth, even in small ways.

Juggling It All: The Breaking Point as a Springboard

College soon became a relentless balancing act. I was working at a bank, playing sports, and studying civil engineering, each demanding an enormous amount of time and effort. Unlike many of my classmates whose tuition was covered by their parents, I had to manage school, work, and athletics all on my own. On top of that, I was on a scholarship that required me to maintain a high GPA. The pressure was suffocating.

Then came an unexpected opportunity: I was invited to join Delta Gamma, a sorority. Up until that point, I had been so focused on academics, my job, and sports that I hadn't made much time for fun. I hadn't realized how much I needed an outlet until I found one. The sorority gave me a sense of community, a way to connect, and a reason to step outside the academic grind. But no matter how much I tried to balance everything, I started burning out. The schedule was brutal: early morning classes, work shifts, studying, and sorority events. It felt like I was drowning. I wasn't performing at my best in my studies or sports. Something had to give.

After a lot of internal debate, I made one of the hardest decisions of my college career: I quit playing sports for the university. It felt like a loss at first, a breakdown of an identity I cherished. I had spent years defining myself as an athlete, and suddenly, that part of me was gone. But deep down, I knew I had to make the sacrifice. Engineering was my priority, and I couldn't afford to be spread so thin. This setback, this difficult season of burnout, became a springboard. Letting go of sports allowed me to fully commit to my studies and my job at the bank. That decision taught me an important lesson about resilience: it's not just about pushing through, it's also about the gritty, messy, yet powerful act of knowing when to pivot and choose a path aligned with a deeper truth.

Finding Unexpected Strength and Leading Authentically

Just as I was settling into my new routine, a girl from my dorm found out I had quit. She encouraged me to try out for the rugby team. Rugby? I had never played before. I had thrown a football a few times, sure, but I had no idea how to play rugby. I didn't know the rules, the strategy, nothing. But something in me said, *Why not?* What started as a spontaneous decision turned into something I genuinely loved. Rugby became my stress relief and my way to stay active without the grueling schedule of my previous sports. It allowed me to stay connected to athletics, but on my own terms.

Meanwhile, I was still navigating the challenges of being a woman in engineering. There were moments I questioned if I had chosen the right path. The coursework was intense, and on top of that, I constantly felt like I didn't belong. Some of my classmates made it clear that I was different, that I didn't fit their mold. Even though I was earning top grades and was part of the Honors program, there was always that unspoken feeling of *I don't belong here.* But I did. I worked hard. I had earned my place. And I wasn't about to let anyone take that away from me.

I knew I couldn't do it alone, though. I started looking for places where I *did* belong. That's when I noticed a bulletin board in the engineering building listing various student organizations, including The Society of Civil Engineers and the Society of Women Engineers. I figured if I was struggling, others probably were too. So, I joined. And it changed everything. I found a network of people who shared the same struggles and faced similar obstacles. I built friendships that would last long beyond college. I became more involved, and eventually, I was elected President of the Society of Women Engineers, leading from a place of shared experience and authentic connection rather than a predefined leadership mold. Some of my board members were men, and many of them remain close friends to this day. Those extracurricular activities became more than just something to put on a résumé. They were a

*lifeline. They helped me step outside the relentless
academic pressure, meet people who inspired me, and
give back to the community in ways I never expected.*

*Looking back, my college experience was defined by
constant adjustments. I had to learn when to push
forward and when to pivot, when to speak up and
when to listen, when to take on more and when to let
go. Resilience wasn't just about enduring challenges; it
was about adapting to them, using setbacks as
springboards to clarity about what truly mattered. I
faced self-doubt, burnout, and isolation. But every
setback forced me to find another way forward, to
grow from the gritty experiences. I didn't just survive
those years, I thrived. I proved to myself that I could
handle the unknown, carve my own path, and come out
stronger on the other side. College wasn't just about
getting a degree. It was about learning what I was
capable of. It was about resilience in action.*

Michele's Story - Resilience Isn't Pretty, But It's Powerful: Leading Through Storms

*Resilience used to be a word I associated purely with
strength, forward motion, and grit. But I now know it
also means rebuilding, surrendering, and sometimes,*

falling apart just enough to begin again. It's the epitome of something gritty, messy, and incredibly powerful. While Melissa's journey through college showed how strength is built in early adulthood, my own lessons in resilience came years later, when life, leadership, and personal identity collided all at once.

From the outside, I looked like I had it all: a thriving career, a beautiful family, a strong sense of self. But behind closed doors, I was navigating a storm I didn't see coming. I was in the middle of a divorce that shook the foundation of my world, fighting for custody of my two-year-old, and working under a toxic, power-hungry boss who made every workday a battle. Oh—and I was leading a division of more than 2,000 employees. I was only 29 years old, and I didn't just feel like I was failing. I felt like I was drowning. It wasn't the kind of fear I had known before. It was heavier. Sharper. It followed me everywhere—into boardrooms, into bedtime routines with my kid, into the silence between sobs in my car before walking into the house. But here's what I've learned: real resilience doesn't happen when life is going well. It's born in the chaos. It's refined in the mess.

The Illusion of Having It All Together

I was "supposed" to be the strong one. The leader. The mother who kept it together. The boss who showed up with strategy and solutions. The woman who didn't break down under pressure. But the truth was—I was barely holding it together. There were mornings I'd walk into work with mascara smudged from crying in traffic. I'd lead back-to-back meetings while secretly fielding texts from lawyers. I was holding an entire division up on one shoulder, and my personal life on the other. Picture a circus act where the juggler is also the tightrope walker, fire-breather, and occasionally the one cleaning up elephant poop—yeah, that was me. Graceful wasn't the word. But persistent? Abso-f-ing-lutely.

No one teaches you how to survive when your personal life collapses at the same time your professional responsibilities reach an all-time high. There is no manual for such a delicate balancing act. And to be honest, I didn't balance it—I wobbled my way through it, one breath, one boundary, one brutally honest conversation at a time. I learned quickly that pretending was too heavy to carry. Resilience, for me, began the moment I stopped trying to perform perfectly and allowed myself to be real. This difficult season, this breakdown of my carefully constructed life, became an unexpected springboard.

When Survival Meets Leadership: Leading from Truth

Leading others while struggling to lead myself was one of the greatest challenges I've ever faced. There were days I questioned everything—my competence, my voice, my choices. But something powerful happened in that season.

Because I was stripped of my armor, I started leading from truth, not from title. I became more human, more transparent, more attuned to others. I realized that people don't want perfect leaders—they want present ones. I stopped pretending to be unbreakable and started leading with empathy. I was no longer afraid to say, "I don't have the answer right now," or "I'm having a hard day too". And ironically, that's when my leadership became most effective. That's when I started to build not just a career, but a legacy. People started opening up more. They leaned in. Because I wasn't performing, I was genuinely connecting. My rawness became a bridge. My mess became a mirror for others. I began to understand that being real was my superpower, not a liability.

The Break Was the Breakthrough

That season of my life felt like a complete unraveling—but in hindsight, it was a necessary breaking, a difficult period that ultimately propelled growth. I was forced to reevaluate who I was and what I truly wanted. I made a decision: I was going to rebuild—but this time, on my terms. I stopped chasing approval from toxic authority figures. I redefined success as peace over prestige. I gave myself permission to ask for help, to slow down, to say no. I started listening to my body, my intuition, my truth. And I got very clear about the kind of environments I would never tolerate again. I stopped trying to "bounce back" and instead gave myself permission to grow forward. To rise differently. And to never again confuse resilience with silence.

And if you ever find yourself wondering if you're strong enough to survive what feels impossible, remember this: I once doubted everything. I questioned if I could rise again. But I did, not as the same version of me, but as someone stronger, softer, wiser, and more aligned. Resilience, in the end, isn't about the clean comeback. It's about the courage to rebuild—even when the blueprint has gone missing and you're standing in the rubble holding a hammer, a cup of coffee, and a few battle scars. It's gritty, it's powerful, and it's yours.

The Strength in the Stretch: Resilience as a Practice

As our stories show, resilience isn't a one-time decision; it's a series of choices, a continuous becoming. It's about consistently choosing truth over image, pivoting when needed, and resting when necessary. Resilience is a muscle built in real time, not in the glossy aftermath, but in the gritty middle. It's forged in the difficult conversations you didn't want to have, in the boundaries you were scared to set, in the moments no one applauded but you showed up for yourself anyway.

It's built when you tell the truth, even when your voice shakes, when you give yourself permission to pause without shame, and when you stop proving and start honoring what you actually need. Because the truth is, resilience isn't always loud. Sometimes it looks like staying. Sometimes it looks like leaving. Sometimes it's doing nothing for a while, just so you can finally hear yourself again.

And here's the radical part: resilience doesn't have to be proven to anyone else. It only has to be real for *you*. You don't owe your strength a performance. You owe it your presence. This understanding is key to leading from your truth, not just a title or an expectation.

Key Takeaways for Resilience in Action:

- True resilience is gritty and often messy; it's about adapting and learning through challenges, not just silently enduring them.
- Setbacks, breakdowns, and difficult seasons, while painful, are often powerful springboards for profound clarity, growth, and re-evaluation of what truly matters.
- Leading from your truth, embracing vulnerability and authenticity, is more impactful than leading from a title or performing a role, especially during challenging times.
- Resilience involves knowing when to pivot, rest, or ask for help, not just pushing through until you break.

Reflective Questions:

Think of a significant setback or difficult season in your life. How did that experience, in hindsight, become a springboard for clarity or growth?

_____

_____

_____

_____

In what situations do you feel pressured to "perform" resilience rather than authentically navigate your challenges? What's one step you can take to show up with more truth in such a situation?

_____

_____

_____

_____

How can you practice leading more from your personal truth (your values, your experiences, your intuition) rather than from external expectations or a formal title this week?

_____

_____

_____

_____

CHAPTER 4

Dismantling the Leadership Mold

"Don't compromise yourself. You are all you've got." —Janis Joplin

---

For generations, leadership has been presented in a rather narrow, often masculine frame. We've been shown images of authority, decisiveness (often without expressed vulnerability), and a certain kind of command. But what if that mold doesn't fit? What if it never truly did, especially for women who bring a diverse array of strengths and styles to the table? This chapter is about breaking free from that rigid mold. It's about recognizing that there is no single "right" way to lead, live, or rise. There's just *your* way.

That's what being a Maverick is all about, not rebellion for the sake of noise, but courageous alignment with your authentic self. It's the decision to stop molding yourself to fit into outdated systems and start redesigning the system, or at least your interaction with it around who you truly are.

But this isn't easy, especially for women. According to Deloitte's Women @ Work 2023 report, nearly 60% of women feel they can't be fully themselves at work. More than half feel pressure to tone down their authenticity just to be taken seriously. And among women in leadership? The majority say they feel constantly judged for how they show up, too bold, too soft, too much, or not enough. The pressure to conform is relentless. Which is why choosing your own voice, your unique leadership style, is revolutionary.

Being your own Maverick, and thus dismantling old leadership molds, means stepping out of the box entirely. It means questioning the metrics, rewriting the rules where you can, and creating impact on your own terms, not to be different, but to be honest, because the most powerful woman in the room isn't always the loudest or the one who fits the traditional image. She's the one who's most aligned, leading from her core with her unique blend of vision, confidence, empathy, and yes, even imperfection.

Melissa's Story — Choosing Myself Over the Hustle: Forging a Unique Path

Fear holds us back from nearly everything we want in life! We fear applying for the job, moving to a new city, taking the leap on that dream trip, or starting the business that lives rent-free in our imagination. Fear is biologically wired into our brains to protect us; our amygdala signals danger, even when the threat isn't real. That's the tricky part: our brain doesn't distinguish between actual risk and imagined failure. Uncertainty can feel terrifying. When we can't predict or control what's coming, we hesitate. But we can build bridges over that fear by asking: *What's the worst that could happen, and could I live through it?*

Unlearning the Life Checklist

Now let's talk about an outdated philosophy: the life checklist. You know the one I'm talking about: graduate college, get a good job, find a partner, have kids, buy a house, and chase a "happy" life according to a timeline someone else invented. I believed in that checklist. I set all the milestone dates. I thought I had to hit each one or fall behind. Funny enough, I wrote a book in my 20s. But I didn't publish it. I told myself, *What do I know at 25?* Looking back, I had plenty to say. I just didn't trust my voice – yet a crucial element of authentic leadership.

What I've learned is this: life doesn't care about your perfect plan. It happens on its own terms, whether you're ready or not. And if you're not paying attention, it has a funny way of handing you the same lesson over and over again, like dating the same wrong guy in a different jacket, or working for a different version of the bad boss you swore you'd never tolerate again. That's why owning your Maverick nature matters. A Maverick is someone who becomes aware of who they are becoming and asks whether life is handing them déjà vu because they haven't yet grown into their next chapter, perhaps by breaking a mold they've been stuck in.

Leading Without the Rulebook

So, I ask you: Are you living your best life or just the one you fell into? Are you becoming the person you set out to be, or did you get lost along the way, trying to fit a prescribed leadership style? Being a Maverick means grabbing the bull by the horns (yes, I'm a Texan now) and making things happen, often in your own unique way. I still remember my grandfather's advice: *Focus on what's most important right now.* Back then, it was school. That wisdom has stayed with me through every chapter. It reminds me to go all in on what matters, my work, my growth, my mission, while trusting that the rest will catch up in time. We can't be everything to everyone, all the time. And we don't have to be.

Every time I've pivoted careers and there have been many, I've had to lean in fully, embracing imperfection and learning as I went. I read everything I could. I showed up in person. I shook hands. I watched what made people tick. I didn't clock in and wait for success to find me. Some days took twelve hours. Others took eight. But Mavericks don't do average, and they don't wait for permission to lead in their own style. They commit. They fall. They learn. They rise. Yes, I've made the same mistake more than once. But third time's the charm, and every stumble has taught me something worth knowing, refining my own approach rather than trying to emulate a flawless, rigid ideal.

Betting on the Unexpected

My journey into the casino gaming industry is a testament to this. I was in the thick of my civil engineering career, working long hours, managing large, complex projects, and checking all the boxes of what I thought "success" was supposed to look like. On paper, everything made sense. But in my gut? I knew I wanted something more, something different, I just didn't know what that was yet. One day, a close friend reached out and said, "Melissa, just apply. This job is made for you." I trusted her, so I clicked the link, didn't bother to look at the company name, uploaded my resume, and hit submit.

Then the phone rang. "Is this Melissa?"

"Yes..."

"This is HR calling about your application."

I was completely caught off guard. Gaming what? I had zero idea what the company was or what I had applied for. But something in the caller's kind, calm, and confident voice made me stay on the line. I decided to take the interview.

When I walked away from civil engineering and into the casino gaming industry, people in my world were stunned. Zero people supported me. "Wait, you're doing what now?"

But my inner Maverick – oh, she was alive and well. She whispered, *They don't have to get it. You're not looking for permission, you're looking for your path.* And maybe I didn't have all the answers. Maybe it was a risk. But I knew I was ready to bet on myself, to lead myself into the unknown. I had no experience in gaming, zero contacts, and wasn't sure I belonged. But I kept showing up. I asked the hard questions. I learned fast. I worked hard. And because I said yes to that one unexpected interview, trusting my own imperfect process over a pre-defined career ladder, I've been trusted to lead global initiatives and collaborate with brilliant minds.

Sometimes, the best chapters of your life, and the most authentic expressions of your leadership, begin with a phone call you never expected and a version of you that dared to say yes to your own unique path. When you listen to that inner Maverick, the part of you that's bold enough to leap before you feel ready, you don't just get a new job. You step into a new identity. You take back your power. You begin to live and lead intentionally, not accidentally.

Michele's Story — I Stopped Asking for Permission: Redefining My Leadership

For so long, I wore every hat. The achiever. The perfectionist. The fixer. The one who didn't just rise to expectations—she crushed them. But I was performing a version of myself that looked powerful from the outside but didn't feel whole on the inside. My true Maverick moment, the moment I started to dismantle the leadership mold I had internalized, didn't come in a boardroom or a breakthrough. It came in the quiet decision to stop abandoning myself for approval.

I began unlearning the myth that leadership has to look a certain way. That being direct made me cold. That being intuitive made me emotional. That being ambitious made me too much. None of that was true. What's true is this: my leadership doesn't fit a mold. It's mine. I'm not here to maintain the status quo—I'm here to disrupt it, with empathy and vision. My style is direct, intuitive, emotionally intelligent, and deeply human. I challenge with compassion, lead with vision, and coach with fire. I don't sugarcoat—I stir the pot. I'm not performing leadership—I'm redefining it. And when I finally started owning that—when I began leading like me—everything transformed. My business. My impact. My sense of self.

When Ambition Meets Alignment

Becoming your own Maverick doesn't mean being fearless. It means being honest. It means trusting your own voice more than the noise. It means no longer outsourcing your worth. The moment I stopped asking for permission to be myself, to lead in my own way, was the moment I truly became powerful.

I used to treat ambition like a checklist, racing to unlock some kind of cosmic gold star. But I started wondering—who was I collecting these stars for? Saying yes to myself, to my authentic leadership style, meant saying no to the hustle that wore me down—the kind that whispers, "Just one more thing and then you can rest." Spoiler alert: the finish line always moves. I had to stop playing tug-of-war with the person I was told to be and the one I actually am. It was like trying to run a marathon in stilettos—impressive in theory, brutal in execution, and definitely not sustainable. So, I kicked off the heels. I stopped performing and started pacing myself for a life and a leadership approach that felt aligned.

Quiet Power, Bold Path

Here's what no one tells you about choosing yourself and your unique style: It's terrifying at first. There's no applause. No certificate of bravery. Just the quiet knowing that this decision—this one right here—is the one that shifts your future.

I've walked away from titles that impressed strangers but suffocated me. I've had to remind myself, "You're not hard to love, you're just hard to manipulate." And I've built a life, and a way of leading, that doesn't ask me to shrink.

My Maverick isn't loud or rebellious for show. She's precise. She shows up with courage tucked in her back pocket and conviction in her walk. She doesn't wait to be invited to lead—she creates her own seat, paints it gold, and says, "Let's begin."

The Audacity to Be You: Leading on Your Own Terms

You don't need more validation; you need more truth. The kind that disrupts your people-pleasing. The kind that whispers, "You already know who you are." The kind that calls you to rise, not to impress, but to embody your authentic leadership. You don't need to fit in; you need to break through. Through outdated rules. Through performative leadership. Through the internalized belief that success requires shrinking.

Becoming your own Maverick means claiming your wholeness, owning your complexity, and refusing to be defined by leadership templates that were never made for you. It means understanding that leading differently *is* leadership. That softness can be strength. That fire can be grace. That your power lies in how deeply you trust your own voice, your own unique blend of empathy, vision, confidence, and even your beautiful imperfections.

The world doesn't need more women trying to fit into a constricting leadership mold; it needs more honest ones. Women who stop contorting to be accepted and start expanding to be free. So don't wait for someone else to name your worth or validate your style. You are already qualified. Already worthy. Already whole. Lead like you. Live like you. Rise like you. Because *you* are the revolution.

Key Takeaways for Dismantling the Leadership Mold:

- True leadership isn't about conforming to a rigid, outdated mold; it's about courageous alignment with your authentic self, even if it looks different.

- Owning your unique style, your blend of intuition, empathy, directness, vision, confidence, and imperfection, is your most powerful leadership tool.
- Redefine leadership on your own terms by trusting your voice, valuing your unique experiences, and being willing to step away from paths or expectations that don't serve your truth.
- The journey to authentic leadership involves embracing honesty over fearlessness and choosing internal validation over external approval.

Reflective Questions:

Where are you currently trying to fit into a leadership "mold" that doesn't feel authentic to you? What's one way you could express your unique style more fully this week?

What qualities (e.g., empathy, intuition, directness, vision, collaboration) do you consider part of your unique leadership strengths, even if they don't fit traditional definitions? How can you leverage them more?

_____

_____

_____

_____

What "permission" are you waiting for to lead in a way that feels more true to yourself? What might happen if you stopped waiting and simply chose to lead from your core?

_____

_____

_____

_____

CHAPTER 5

Alignment Over Achievement

"When you know yourself, you are empowered. When you accept yourself, you are invincible." —Tina Lifford

---

Who are you when the titles fall away? It's a question that a few of us, especially women, are encouraged to explore deeply. From early on, we're often praised for achievement, not authenticity, for what we *do*, not who we *are*. But when your identity is primarily built on performance, external validation, or the relentless pursuit of the next milestone, success, even when attained, can feel like a hollow shell. And over time, that shell inevitably cracks.

In a world that rewards constant output and visible accomplishments, it's easy to lose sight of our inner compass. An IBM Women in Leadership Report found that only 1 in 5 women in leadership feel fully authentic at work. That number drops even further for women of color, LGBTQ+ professionals, and those in male-dominated industries. Why? Because, for too long, conformity has been presented as the cost of access. We adapt, we filter, we contort ourselves to meet expectations, only to sometimes feel like impostors in rooms we've rightfully earned our way into.

But here's the liberating truth we want to explore in this chapter: True identity isn't something you achieve through performance; it's something you return to, something you *are*. When your goals are built on someone else's definition of success or purely on external achievements, even your biggest wins can feel empty. This is the core of misalignment. However, when your ambitions are anchored in who you really are, your values, your purpose, your authentic self, something profound shifts. You stop chasing applause and start aligning with what genuinely fulfills you. This is the heart of purpose-driven living. The real success story isn't about doing more; it's about becoming more *you*, and leading a life and a career that feels truly yours.

Melissa's Story — Aligned or Exhausted: The Power of Leading from Your Core

Growing up, my identity was tied closely to performance, sports, academics, and the quiet pressure to prove I was smart enough, tough enough, and driven enough. My younger brother and I were raised with a clear sense of purpose. Our dad treated school and sports like our first job. He believed that if we could excel in the classroom and on the field, we'd learn how to lead, how to show up for a team, and how to face challenges head-on. Discipline and grit were non-negotiable.

But what shaped me just as deeply, maybe even more, was my mom's influence. She was the kind of woman who gave freely, without expecting anything in return. Our house was often filled with people who needed a warm meal, a place to stay, or a fresh start. Looking back, I realize that she didn't just teach kindness, she lived it. Her lessons were about character, not accomplishment: the importance of good manners, humility, honesty, and allowing us to fail so we could grow. She showed me that success without generosity isn't really success at all.

Those values became part of me before I ever realized they were shaping my identity. As I grew older and moved out on my own, I found myself doing the same thing: opening my home, offering support, creating space for others to get back on their feet. It wasn't a conscious choice. It was instinct. My identity wasn't just something I was building; it was something I was returning to, a blueprint handed down by my parents, one part drive, one part heart.

Success Without Self is Empty

I've also learned what it feels like when you're not aligned with your true self. You can be doing all the right things on paper, earning promotions, collecting praise, hitting milestones, and still feel empty. When your goals are driven by the achievement of external expectations instead of authenticity, success begins feeling like a performance. You're showing up, but not as yourself. It becomes a cycle of burnout, overthinking, and self-doubt. Even in your brightest moments, there's that whisper: "Is this really me?"

I've lived that tension. I've chased validation, focused solely on achievement, instead of purpose. And it left me more disconnected than ever. That kind of misalignment doesn't just exhaust you, it chips away at your confidence, because deep down, you know you're not living from a place of truth. You're meeting other people's standards, not your own. And over time, that takes a toll.

Lead With Who You Are

For a long time, I thought success meant reaching the next goalpost: a better job, bigger title, louder applause. But with time (and a few stumbles), I started to see things differently. When I led from my identity, when my values showed up in my goals, that's when things started to click. That's when success felt real and sustainable. I stopped striving for approval and achievement for achievement's sake and started leading with alignment. And that changed everything.

I've learned that your identity isn't what you do. It's who you are when the titles fade and the pressure quiets. It's how you treat people when no one's watching. And when your goals grow from that place of authenticity, they aren't just about getting ahead; they become about bringing others along with you, building something meaningful, and staying true to yourself along the way. Because when you lead with identity, success doesn't just follow; it finds you when you're ready.

The Power of Inner Alignment

Today, I make decisions differently. I no longer measure success by how busy I am or how polished my resume looks. I measure it by impact. Am I helping others rise? Am I creating space where people feel seen, safe, and supported? Am I leading in a way that my mom would be proud of and my younger self would recognize? The answer isn't always perfect, but it's honest. And that honesty, that alignment between who I am and what I do, is where the magic happens.

Success has become a byproduct, not the pursuit. And the deeper I trust my identity to guide me, the more fulfilled I become, not just in work, but in life. As Brené Brown once said, "Authenticity is the daily practice of letting go of who we think we're supposed to be and embracing who we are". And when you do that, when you finally align with your true self, something shifts. The right people stay. The energy vampires, the ones who drain your light, naturally fall away. What's left is clarity, peace, and the kind of success that doesn't require you to lose yourself to find it.

And here's the beautiful part: when you're living in alignment, it's almost like getting a shot of caffeine for your soul. That kind of authenticity gives you energy not just to keep going, but to go further with more joy, more intention, and more connection. It fuels creativity, strengthens your boundaries, and recharges your purpose. You wake up excited, not just about what you do, but about who you are while doing it.

Alignment doesn't mean everything gets easier, but it does make everything feel lighter. Because when your life and work reflect your identity, you're no longer pushing against the current, you're moving with it. That's where the real momentum begins. That's where sustainable success and peace live.

Michele's Story — Who Are You Without the Title? Finding Purpose Beyond Performance

I've had seasons where I built an identity around what I did, not who I was. My titles, my roles, the way others introduced me—those became my markers of worth, my primary achievements. I had a bio that sparkled and a calendar that groaned under the weight of importance. But then life did what it does best: it stripped away the noise.

Motherhood shook me to my core. Not because I didn't love it, but because I had spent years building a life that didn't make space for who I was outside of achievement. When I paused my career to raise my preemie twins, I didn't just hit pause on work—I hit pause on the version of me that only knew how to be productive. It was like going from high heels and boardrooms to spit-up and white noise machines overnight. It forced me to meet myself again, stripped of performance and accolades. Suddenly, there were no meetings to lead, no awards to chase—just quiet, unrelenting moments of real life. And in those moments, I discovered a new kind of strength, a purpose far removed from professional accomplishment.

The Soul Always Knocks

I've also faced career crossroads where walking away from something I had worked hard for felt like failure. It's wild how identity can feel like Velcro—every title and trophy sticking to you until you don't know where you end and your LinkedIn profile begins. But what I realized was this: every time I stepped closer to my truth, I redefined success. Not by income. Not by influence. But by integrity and a 360° IMPACT.

There were moments when choosing alignment meant disappointing others—saying no to a promotion, leaving a leadership role, turning down offers that looked like "dream jobs" on paper. It's like being handed a beautifully wrapped gift and realizing there's nothing inside that fits you. But every time I honored who I really was, I gained something far more valuable: clarity, peace, and power.

Choosing alignment doesn't always feel like a mountaintop moment. Sometimes it feels like sitting in your car, staring at your phone, rehearsing how to say "no" without setting the whole world on fire. But saying no to what dims your light, to achievements that don't align with your purpose, is the first step to fully stepping into what sets you ablaze.

I've had to get honest about my own patterns, too. The hustle, the people-pleasing, the overachieving—all clever disguises for fear. Fear of not being enough without the applause of achievement. Fear that if I wasn't producing, I was somehow losing. But here's what I've learned: you can't fake alignment. You can dress it up. You can pretend to love the grind. You can wear the blazer, lead the call, post the highlight reel—but eventually, your soul will knock. Loudly. And no title is thick enough to muffle that sound.

Alignment Over Achievement Alone

Today, I don't chase alignment; I choose it. And I teach others to do the same. Because success defined purely by achievement without identity isn't success—it's self-abandonment.

Alignment is waking up and recognizing yourself in the mirror—not just in your reflection, but in your values, your words, your work. It's being able to look at your calendar and say, "Yeah, that looks like me".

I've redefined what a powerful woman looks like. She doesn't just climb ladders for the sake of climbing. She builds tables. She doesn't just collect titles. She creates space. She doesn't just perform. She leads with purpose. And now? I'm still ambitious. Still driven. Still showing up with bold goals and a big vision. But the biggest win? I no longer abandon myself to get there. Because alignment isn't the absence of ambition; it's ambition with a soul.

The Power of Returning to Yourself: Choosing Alignment Over Hustle

As we've both discovered, and as we see in countless women we work with, authenticity is a leadership skill.

Alignment is a performance strategy—a strategy for achieving sustainable high performance, that is. And identity is the root system of sustainable success. Because without identity, without that deep connection to your authentic self, achievements can feel hollow. You can hit every milestone, climb every ladder, and still feel unfulfilled if you're doing it in a costume that doesn't fit. This is the core difference between a life driven by the hustle for external achievement and one guided by internal alignment and purpose.

But the more you lead from who you truly are, the less noise you tolerate. You stop chasing applause and start honoring alignment. You stop shape-shifting to fit in and start expanding into spaces that reflect your truth. You become clearer. Bolder. Louder when it matters. Quieter when it doesn't. And your presence? It begins to speak even when you're silent.

Success is no longer about climbing for the sake of the climb; it's about coming home. To your values. To your voice. To your version of power. Because the goal was never to become someone else; it was always to become *more you*. When you learn to lead with internal alignment and not just external hustle, you build a life that truly feels like your own.

Key Takeaways for Alignment Over Achievement:

- A performance-based identity, focused solely on external achievements, often leads to a hollow sense of success; purpose-driven living stems from aligning with your authentic self and core values.
- Chasing someone else's version of success or prioritizing achievements that don't align with your truth can be a form of self-abandonment; recognizing this is the first step to stopping.
- Leading with alignment means making conscious choices rooted in your identity and purpose, which fuels sustainable energy, joy, and impact, rather than relying on relentless hustle.
- True fulfillment comes when your ambitions and actions are an authentic expression of who you are, not just what you do.

Reflective Questions:

In what areas of your life are you driven more by external achievements or performance, and where are you driven by internal purpose and alignment? What's one small shift you could make?

When have you felt you were chasing someone else's version of success? What were the signs, and what did it take (or would it take) to stop?

What does "leading with alignment, not hustle" mean to you personally? How could practicing this change the way you approach your goals or daily life?

What does a life that truly "feels like yours" look like? What core values are at its center?

_____

_____

_____

_____

CHAPTER 6

Stronger Together

"Surround yourself with only people who are going to lift you higher."
—Oprah Winfrey

You were never meant to do this alone. We've been sold a myth of lone-wolf success, the idea that independence is the ultimate strength, that real leaders don't ask for help, and that the highest achievers carry the weight solo. But the truth, as we've both learned profoundly, is that isolation isn't strength. It's slow erosion.

Meaningful community and connection are not just nice-to-haves; they are essential to thriving. According to a study by the American Psychological Association, chronic loneliness is now considered a public health crisis, especially for women in leadership. Despite being surrounded by people, one in three women leaders says they feel consistently unsupported and alone. That isn't just an emotional burden; it's a professional one. Research from the Center for Talent Innovation found that women with strong peer networks and access to mentorship are two times more likely to advance into leadership roles and report higher levels of confidence and clarity.

Community isn't a luxury. It's a leadership imperative. It's the circle that grounds us in truth, reflects who we are becoming, and stretches us to rise beyond what we thought possible. But here's the catch: community isn't found, it's built. You build it by being real. By asking. By showing up even when you're not at your best. It starts the moment you stop performing and start inviting. The most resilient women aren't the ones who have all the answers. They're the ones who know who to call when they don't. Success rarely happens in isolation; it grows and is sustained in community.

Melissa's Story — Stronger Together: Finding My People

Community didn't click for me right away. Like many of us early in our careers, I tried to "eat the elephant in one bite," focusing on climbing the ladder, checking the boxes, and pushing forward solo. After graduation, I stayed active in the communities I knew, like the Society of Civil Engineers, the Society of Women Engineers, and Delta Gamma. But something was missing. In college, volunteering had filled my cup; it gave me purpose beyond the classroom. After college, those opportunities were harder to find, and I didn't realize just how much I missed them.

Let's talk about the other side of not building community, the part no one posts about. The loneliness. The disconnection. The feeling of having no one to turn to. I know from experience that it's not a place you want to stay in. When I first moved to Reno, Nevada, for college, I had a few casual acquaintances from high school, but none I felt close enough to ask for help moving into my dorm. That moment hit me hard: if I needed help, I had no one. It was the original catalyst that pushed me to start showing up, joining clubs, and meeting new people. I wanted to rebuild the kind of community I had in Las Vegas, where my family and friends didn't just cheer me on; they *showed up*. Every move I made growing up, they were there, packing, driving, lifting, and laughing alongside me. What could take someone weeks or even months to unpack and settle, we handled in two days flat because we had each other. I craved that same support system in this new chapter of my life.

Finding Belonging Without a Title

That's when I found my way into a volunteer network committed to giving back. It gave me a new space to grow personally, not just professionally. I didn't have to lead with my resume or talk about my job title. I could just be and contribute in a way that fed my soul. Over time, I served in three JL chapters, Reno, Las Vegas, and Austin, and with each move, my community deepened. As someone who's logged more hours at Starbucks than most remote workers (and has the gold stars to prove it), I have to quote Howard Schultz, former CEO of Starbucks: "When you're surrounded by people who share a passionate commitment around a common purpose, anything is possible". That's exactly what I found. What started as a side interest became something much bigger. I caught the "community bug" and continued building across various sectors, including nonprofits, athletic teams, education, hospitality, and executive networks. What I didn't realize at the time was that I was intentionally building relationships that fueled my purpose and creating a rich, resilient network that extended far beyond my career.

The Power of Intentional Gathering

If you're someone who doesn't have an "in case of emergency" person, this is your sign. It's time to shift your energy into making a friend. Start with what you love. Find people who share that interest. Shared passions create natural places for connection, and conversation flows more easily when you're already on common ground.

In the words of Priya Parker, author of *The Art of Gathering*, "The way we gather matters. It matters because how we gather is how we live". And for me, gathering with intention has been a cornerstone of living fully and leading meaningfully.

Looking back now, I see that these communities, these people have brought more joy, wisdom, and opportunity into my life than I ever expected. In a world that can feel increasingly transactional, choose to be someone who builds meaningful, fun, and intentional relationships *before* you need them.

Because of those connections, I've had experiences I couldn't have imagined: dinners with presidents, conversations with pro athletes and CEOs, collaborations with founders and banks. The moments were many, but the real magic was in the people. As Jean Case, former chair of National Geographic, said: "We are stronger when we cheer each other on". And

I've come to learn that success doesn't happen in isolation. It grows in community.

Michele's Story — Built by the Women Beside Me: The Power of Collective Rising

For years, I believed leadership was about strength, and strength meant not needing anyone. I wore my independence like armor. But the truth? I was exhausted. When I launched my business, I tried to do everything alone. I thought asking for help would make me seem unqualified. I held it all, quietly drowning under the weight of expectations. It wasn't sustainable. Picture this: I was like a one-woman band at a parade—clashing cymbals, playing the trumpet, beating the drum, and somehow still waving to the crowd with a smile. Exhausted. Out of sync. But too proud to ask someone else to carry a beat. That was me—leading solo, proudly stubborn, and secretly overwhelmed.

The shift came when I began intentionally building a network, not for business gain, but for real support. Women who got it. Coaches who challenged me. Organizations that were aligned with my mission. Friends who didn't need the polished version of me to show up. They didn't flinch at my mess; they made space for it. The kind of space that is sacred. This was about intentionally building relationships that fueled my purpose and my well-being.

Nurture Over Networking Always

I learned that real community isn't built on business cards or happy-hour selfies. It's built on the courage to say, "I'm not okay today". On the generosity of sharing resources without expecting anything back. On group texts that say, "You've got this," when you're questioning everything, and the kind of belly laughs that should count as therapy. Community isn't something you stumble into. It's something you create through honesty, consistency, and vulnerability. It's built one brave conversation at a time. And it grows not from networking, but from nurturing.

These women have helped me pivot, rebuild, and expand. They've brought ideas to life, reminded me to rest, and shown up in ways that don't make the highlight reel—but absolutely make the difference. If building a business is like baking bread (and trust me, it often feels like one big yeasty science experiment), then community is the yeast. Without it, things don't rise. They just sit there, flat, heavy, and hard to digest.

Let People Help You Rise

I've learned that my strength doesn't come from holding it all. It comes from letting go. Letting people in. Letting myself be seen—flaws, fears, brilliance, and all. I don't rise because I have it all figured out. I rise because I'm surrounded by people who remind me, I don't have to do it alone.

This is the essence of why connection is essential to thriving. So, if you're in the middle of trying to be everything for everyone—pause. Take a breath. Text a friend. Join the group. Accept the invite. Let someone in!

Because true leadership isn't about doing it all; it's about knowing when to link arms with the people who'll help you carry the load—and maybe even make you laugh through it. And if you're fortunate, they'll also bring wine or ice cream when you need it the most. Which, let's be honest, is the cornerstone of every great support system.

The Circle That Carries You: Cultivating True Belonging

Let's be honest: we all crave connection. But too many of us have been burned by surface-level networking, transactional mentorship, or performative connections that appear impressive on LinkedIn but leave us feeling empty in real life. What we truly need is belonging. The kind that doesn't ask us to shrink. The kind that holds space for our ambition *and* our vulnerability. The kind that doesn't need us to earn our place, but reminds us we already belong.

Because a true community isn't built on perfection, it's built on presence. On truth-telling. On showing up even when you're unsure, overwhelmed, or unpolished. It's built on mutual rise, not silent competition.

So here's your challenge, from us to you: Stop auditioning. Start aligning. Start intentionally building circles that celebrate your wholeness, not just your wins. Relationships that stretch you, support you, and mirror back the woman you're becoming, not the role you're trying to maintain. Because you don't rise alone. You rise *with*. And when you rise in community, you don't just grow, you become unshakable. Success, indeed, doesn't happen in isolation.

Key Takeaways for Being Stronger Together:

- Meaningful community and connection are not optional extras; they are fundamental to our well-being, growth, and ability to thrive, especially for women navigating complex leadership paths.
- Intentionally build relationships rooted in authenticity, shared purpose, and mutual support, rather than focusing solely on transactional networking; these are the connections that truly fuel your journey.
- Success is a collective endeavor; embracing vulnerability and allowing yourself to be supported by a trusted circle will make you stronger and more resilient than trying to achieve everything in isolation.

Reflective Questions:

Where in your life do you feel a strong sense of community and connection? Where do you crave more?

What is one intentional step you can take this week to nurture an existing relationship or build a new connection that could fuel your purpose (not just your professional network)?

_____

_____

_____

_____

Reflect on a time when community support was crucial for you. How can you "pay forward" that kind of support to someone in your circle?

_____

_____

_____

_____

CHAPTER 7

One Bold Yes

"When you learn how much you're worth,
you'll stop giving people discounts."
—Elaine Welteroth

Many of us are handed a "life checklist" early on, a sequence of expected milestones: graduate, get the "right" job, find a partner, climb the ladder. We diligently tick off boxes, often believing this prescribed path is the route to security and happiness. But what happens when your gut whispers of a different journey? What if the unexpected path, the one not on any checklist, holds the key to your most authentic life and truest success? This chapter is about the courage to say "yes" to that unexpected path, often starting with one bold decision.

Risk, in this context, isn't about recklessness; it's about alignment in motion. Some of the boldest career and life moves women make don't begin with absolute certainty. They often begin with a discomfort, a nudge, that quiet yet persistent inner voice whispering: *This isn't it.* It's the knowing that something greater, something more *you*, lies on the other side of fear, if only you're willing to leap.

But leaping doesn't always come naturally, especially when we've been conditioned to overthink instead of act. Studies show that men will often apply for a job if they meet 60% of the qualifications, but women tend to wait until they meet 100%. This caution, while sometimes wise, can also mean missed opportunities if fear becomes the primary driver of our decisions. Fear is natural, an evolutionary response designed to keep us safe. It will likely be a companion on any journey of significance. The key is to understand that while fear gets a seat, it doesn't get to drive the car. Learning to act *despite* fear is where the magic happens. One small act of courage, one "bold yes" in the face of uncertainty, can radically change the trajectory of your life. And as a 2023 McKinsey study found, women who make intentional career pivots into new industries or roles often report higher long-term satisfaction and confidence than those who stay in misaligned positions "for safety". Risk, embraced with intention, is how reinvention happens.

Melissa's Story — From the Call to the Climb: One Unexpected "Yes"

I heard about a development job from a friend, so I jumped online and applied for a role in engineering and development, a field I was well-versed in. After submitting my application, I let my friend know, expecting to hear back about the next steps. But before she could get back to me, I received an unexpected call from a company in the casino gaming industry. This was a field I had zero experience in. No contacts, no background, nothing. When the HR department asked for Melissa, I initially assumed they had the wrong person or that it was about a different job.

I had two choices: Tell them it was a mix-up and hang up. Or stay on the line and listen. That small moment was a pivot point. I chose option two. The woman on the other end of the phone was warm, engaging, and genuinely excited about the role. She explained the job, and as I listened, I realized it sounded interesting and, more importantly, challenging. I had no prior experience in gaming, but something in me, a flicker of courage, said, Why not? So, I said "yes" to an interview. What's the worst that could happen?

The Interviews: Perseverance Despite Uncertainty

When I arrived for the first interview, I quickly sensed that the two men interviewing me weren't particularly interested. They went through the motions, but their body language and tone made it clear, they weren't convinced I was the right fit. Maybe it was my lack of experience in the industry. Maybe they had already decided on another candidate. Fear and doubt could have easily told me to give up. Still, I followed up with both HR and the interviewers afterward, thanked them for their time, and assumed I wouldn't be hearing back.

A few weeks later, another small "yes" was required. I received a call for a second interview. This time, everything felt different. The energy in the room had shifted. The questions were more thoughtful, the conversation more engaging. By the time I walked out, I knew I had the job. But I also knew something else: I was going to have to work very, very hard to catch up, to learn the industry, and to prove I belonged.

The Offer: The Bold "Yes" to a New Trajectory

Then came the offer. When I heard the salary, my stomach dropped. It was significantly lower than what I had been making in engineering, a very large pay cut. This was a major test. The "life checklist" would have screamed "no!" Fear of financial instability was real. I had another choice: Walk away and return to the comfort and known quantity of what I knew. Or take a leap of faith, say one more bold "yes," and bet on myself. My gut told me to take the job. So I did. I took the risk, understanding it was a deviation from any expected path. I figured if it didn't work out, I could always go back to engineering. But something in me said that this leap, this uncomfortable, uncertain step, was going to lead to something bigger. And it did.

I spent the next several years working nonstop, long days, late nights, and weekends, doing whatever it took to understand the industry. I immersed myself in every aspect of the business, asked questions, studied trends, and put in the extra hours that others weren't willing to. There was no shortcut, no easy way to bridge the gap between where I started and where I needed to be. The only way forward was through grit, effort, and an unshakable commitment to learning. It wasn't easy, but I refused to let my lack of experience define me. I knew that if I worked hard enough, I could build the expertise, the network, and the credibility to excel. And that's exactly what I did. That one initial "yes" to an unexpected phone call radically changed my life.

Michele's Story — Walking Away to Build Something That Didn't Exist Yet: A Courageous "Yes" to Self

Some risks are strategic. Others are survival. Mine was both. I didn't start my business because I hated the corporate world. Quite the opposite—I loved the structure, the culture, the rhythm of high-level hospitality. But what I couldn't stomach anymore was poor leadership—the kind that crushes passion, dehumanizes teams, and parades arrogance as authority. This was a direct challenge to my values, pushing me off any "checklist" I might have been on.

My breaking point came in a room full of people I cared deeply about—my team. We were the top-performing region in the company. Highest revenue. Best margins. Most growth potential. And yet, our boss stood there, berating us like we were failures. He didn't criticize the work—he attacked our character! He said our parents should be ashamed of us all. He flaunted his wealth and power like trophies we'd never earn. He told us, flat out: "You'll never become anyone." I kept a straight face in the moment, but inside, something snapped. After the meeting, I gathered the team. I handed them paper and said, "Write down how you feel." They did. Then one by one, each read it out loud and fed the pages into a shredder. This wasn't us destroying our emotions. It was us, unified, taking our power back.

That night, on my drive home, I knew something had to change. Not just around me—within me. I couldn't keep giving my energy to a culture that didn't reflect who I was or what I stood for. So, I made a choice— one bold "yes" to myself and "no" to tolerating the intolerable. I would build the environment I wanted to be part of. And once again, I didn't have a roadmap. Just a fire in my chest and a refusal to let one man's voice define my worth—or that of my team. Fear was present—the fear of the unknown, of financial insecurity, of failure—but the need for alignment was stronger.

Entrepreneurship: The Ultimate "Yes" to an Unexpected Path

Starting your own business is like skydiving with a backpack full of vision and very little else. It is like assembling IKEA furniture blindfolded—no manual, missing screws, but you're determined to make it work. I left behind the comfort of a steady salary, the structure of corporate scaffolding, and the illusion of security. In return, I got uncertainty, sleepless nights, and the terrifying freedom to do things my own way. But what I also got—what made that courageous "yes" all worth it—was impact. The ability to coach leaders into becoming the kind of leaders I wish I'd had. The freedom to say "yes" to the projects that aligned with my soul. The time to be present for my kids, for myself, for life. That's not just entrepreneurship. That's liberation. And it only happened because I was willing to risk everything I'd built... to build something better.

There's no manual for entrepreneurship. In my first year, I said yes to everything, terrified that if I didn't, opportunities would stop coming. In one of my first paid consulting projects, I undercharged by more than 70%—and overdelivered by 150%. The client raved. I lost sleep. And even though it led to referrals, it taught me something invaluable: When you don't know your worth, others will undervalue you, too. That moment hurt, but it sharpened me. It forced me to get clear on my value, to raise my rates, to take up more space. To *build confidence not from external validation, but from integrity and results. And once I owned that? The business grew in ways I never expected. That one bold "yes" to leaving a toxic situation, despite the fear, radically changed my life's trajectory.*

Leaps That Lead to Legacy: The Power of Your "Yes"

As our stories illustrate, risk isn't about knowing exactly how it ends. It's about trusting who you'll become along the way. Every bold move, every courageous "yes" to an unexpected path, opens a door to possibility—not just for you, but for those watching. Your courage creates a ripple. When you take the leap, you give others permission to do the same. You challenge the life checklist. You model what alignment looks like in motion.

Legacy isn't just what you build; it's what your choices, your "yeses," echo in others. The truth is, the path may be unclear. The landing may be bumpy. The rewards may take time. But if the leap, the "yes," is aligned—if it honors who you are and what you believe, even if it's scary—it's always worth it. Because boldness builds more than outcomes, it builds character. It builds clarity. And it builds a future you can stand inside, not just look back on. The right leap, the right "yes," won't always make sense to others, or even to the part of you that craves a predictable checklist. But it will feel like home to you.

Key Takeaways for Your "One Bold Yes":

- True growth often lies off the "life checklist"; be open to saying "yes" to unexpected paths and opportunities, even if they deviate from your original plan.
- Fear is a natural response to uncertainty and risk, but it doesn't have to dictate your decisions; courage is acting in spite of fear.
- One small act of courage, one "bold yes" to an aligned opportunity or a necessary change, can radically reshape your life's trajectory and lead to profound personal and professional growth.
- The most powerful "yeses" often involve betting on yourself and trusting your intuition, even when external circumstances are uncertain or unsupportive.

Reflective Questions:

Is there a "life checklist" you feel you've been consciously or unconsciously following? What's one item on it that no longer feels aligned with who you are or want to become?

Think of a time you said "yes" to something that scared you. What was the outcome, and what did you learn about your own courage?

What is one "bold yes" you are contemplating right now, even if it feels small? What fear is holding you back, and what might be possible if that fear didn't get to drive the decision?

How would your life change if you trusted that one small act of courage today could lead to significant positive shifts in your future?

_____

_____

_____

_____

_____

CHAPTER 8

Unveiling Your Inner Maverick: An Introduction to the 7 Renaissance Woman Archetypes

---

"Owning our story and loving ourselves through that process is the bravest thing that we'll ever do." —Brené Brown

---

Throughout Part I of our journey together, we've explored the essential awakenings of the modern Maverick. We've challenged outdated definitions of success, navigated the landscape of fear, understood the gritty power of resilience, dismantled restrictive leadership molds, prioritized alignment over mere achievement, embraced the strength found in community, and recognized the profound impact of "one bold yes." You've delved into what it means to shed external expectations and begin the return to your authentic self.

Now, as we transition to the next phase of your Renaissance, we want to offer you a powerful lens through which to understand your unique approach to leadership, growth, and transformation more deeply. You are not just one thing. You are not just a leader or a dreamer or a disruptor. You are a mosaic of instincts, values, and lived experiences that shape how you rise, how you lead, and how you evolve.

In our work with hundreds of women through coaching, leadership retreats, and real-life reinventions, we began to notice something: there are patterns. Ways of being. Distinct lenses through which women navigate their Maverick journeys. We call these the 7 Renaissance Woman Archetypes.

These archetypes are not boxes to fit into. They are mirrors. They are designed to help you see your inherent strengths more clearly, claim your unique voice with greater confidence, and unlock the type of momentum that is most natural and potent for *you*. This is not a personality quiz designed to label you; this is a reclamation of self, an invitation to understand and embrace the multifaceted power you already hold.

Here are the 7 Renaissance Woman Archetypes and a glimpse of how they show up in real life:

1. The Visionary Maverick

- Future-Thinker. Big-Dreamer. Possibility Seer.
- You're fueled by what could be. You imagine systems better than the ones you've inherited. You

lead with optimism, depth, and the ability to inspire others into alignment with a new future.

- *Signature Strengths:* Inspiring others, future planning, articulating bold ideas.
- *Watch Out For:* Getting stuck in ideas without grounding them in action.
- *"I've always seen what wasn't there yet and believed in it anyway."*

2. The Builder Maverick

- Structured. Loyal. Legacy-Focused.
- You find deep satisfaction in creating things that last. You're consistent, intentional, and patient. Others may overlook you, but your results speak volumes. You're not flashy, you're foundational.
- *Signature Strengths:* Systems, reliability, sustainable growth.
- *Watch Out For:* Undervaluing innovation or fearing disruption.
- *"I don't just want to win, I want to build something that outlives me."*

3. The Disruptor Maverick

- Rule-Breaker. Provocateur. Change Catalyst.
- You're not here to fit in; you're here to flip the table. You challenge assumptions, question

tradition, and often say what others are afraid to. You're bold, sharp, and unapologetically different.

- *Signature Strengths:* Speaking truth, initiating change, risk-taking.
- *Watch Out For:* Burnout from always pushing boundaries, alienating allies.
- *"If it makes people uncomfortable, it's probably worth doing."*

4. The Connector Maverick

- Relational. Empathetic. Energy-Conscious.
- You lead through people. You build bridges, foster belonging, and know how to read a room better than anyone. You influence with heart, not just with words.
- *Signature Strengths:* Emotional intelligence, trust-building, collaboration.
- *Watch Out For:* Taking on others' emotional labor, losing self in the service of others.
- *"I don't just lead teams, I lead with them."*

5. The Strategist Maverick

- Calculating. Intentional. Quietly Powerful.
- You think ten steps ahead. You analyze, plan, and execute with precision. While others are reacting, you're already building the roadmap. You don't

need the spotlight; you build what others depend on.

- *Signature Strengths:* Problem-solving, pattern recognition, decisive action.
- *Watch Out For:* Overthinking, perfectionism, and analysis paralysis.
- *"I don't need to be loud to be effective. I move when it matters."*

6. The Rebel Maverick

- Intuitive. Bold. Boundary-Breaking.
- You follow your gut. You move fast, speak freely, and shake up the spaces you're in. You don't wait for permission. Your brilliance is your bravery.
- *Signature Strengths:* Quick action, instinctual leadership, confidence.
- *Watch Out For:* Impulsivity, struggling with follow-through.
- *"I leap first. And then I figure it out."*

7. The Alchemist Maverick

- Transformative. Purpose-Driven. Soulful.
- You turn pain into purpose. You feel things deeply and use that wisdom to lead with grace. You're grounded in meaning, guided by intuition, and called to heal or elevate the spaces you're in.

- *Signature Strengths:* Meaning-making, emotional depth, resilience.
- *Watch Out For:* Emotional exhaustion, overextending for others.
- *"My growth didn't come easy, but it came sacred."*

You might see yourself in more than one archetype, and that's the point. You are a spectrum, not a single shade. Use these archetypes as a tool for clarity, for expansion, and for permission. Permission to lead, rise, and build a life that reflects *your* truest version of power.

Your Renaissance begins within. And now, as we prepare to move into Part II: "Embodying Your Inner Maverick," you have a new framework to explore exactly where and how to start. In the chapters that follow, we will dive deep into each of these 7 Maverick Archetypes, providing actionable strategies, insights for navigating challenges, and ways to amplify your innate strengths. Get ready to meet yourself on a whole new level.

PART II

EMBODYING YOUR INNER
MAVERICK

CHAPTER 9

The Visionary Maverick: Illuminating the Path Forward

"I've always seen what wasn't there yet and believed in it anyway."
—The Visionary Maverick

Welcome, Visionary Maverick. You are the one who gazes at the horizon and sees not just what is, but what *could be*. You possess an innate ability to dream beyond the current reality, to imagine systems, solutions, and futures that others may not yet comprehend. You are fueled by possibility, often thinking in expansive, innovative ways. Your leadership is characterized by optimism, a profound sense of depth, and a remarkable capacity to inspire others, painting a compelling picture of a new future that calls them into alignment and action. You don't just dream; you articulate those dreams with a clarity that can ignite movements and transform organizations. You are the architect of tomorrow, driven by an unwavering belief in the potential for something better.

The Light Side:
Your Signature Strengths in Action

As a Visionary Maverick, your power lies in your ability to see beyond the immediate and illuminate the way forward.

- **Inspiring Others:** Your conviction is contagious. When you share your vision, you naturally draw people in. You can articulate complex future states in ways that make them feel not only possible but exciting and achievable.

  - o *In Action:* Imagine a company struggling with outdated processes. You, the Visionary Maverick leader, step in. Instead of just tweaking current methods, you paint a vivid picture of a completely new, streamlined, tech-enabled workflow that not only boosts efficiency but also enhances employee satisfaction and creativity. Your team, initially hesitant about change, becomes energized by your clarity and passion, eager to help build this new reality.

- **Future Planning & Strategic Foresight:** You have a knack for anticipating trends and seeing the long-term implications of current actions (or inactions). This allows you to position yourself, your team, or your organization advantageously for what's to come.

o *In Action:* While others might be focused on quarterly results, you are already conceptualizing the market shifts expected in the next three to five years. You might advocate for investing in nascent technologies or developing skills for future needs, ensuring long-term relevance and success.

- **Articulating Bold Ideas with Clarity:** Your mind generates innovative and often unconventional ideas. Crucially, you can communicate these big-picture concepts in a way that resonates and makes sense, bridging the gap between a lofty vision and relatable understanding.

  o *In Action:* You see a pressing social issue that needs a novel solution. You conceptualize a multi-faceted community initiative that tackles the root causes. You then articulate this vision so compellingly to stakeholders, from potential funders to community members, that they grasp its importance and rally to support it.

The Shadow Side: Potential Pitfalls & "Watch Out For"s

Every strength, when overused or unmanaged, can cast a shadow. For the Visionary Maverick, these are important areas for self-awareness:

- **Getting Stuck in Ideas ("Castles in the Sky" Syndrome):** Your love for ideation can sometimes mean you generate many brilliant concepts but struggle with the practical steps of implementation. The excitement of the *next* idea can overshadow the need to ground the current one.

  o *Manifestation:* Your desk (digital or physical) might be filled with half-finished plans or brilliant concepts that never saw the light of day because the detailed execution felt less inspiring than the initial vision. This can lead to frustration for you and your team if they see a pattern of unfulfilled visions.

- **Impatience with Incremental Progress or Naysayers:** Because you see the future so clearly, you might become frustrated with those who don't grasp your vision immediately or with processes that require slow, steady, incremental change. This can also manifest as underestimating the very real obstacles to implementation.

  o *Manifestation:* You might dismiss valid concerns about resources or timelines as "lack of vision" or become disheartened when practical realities slow down your grand plans. This can sometimes alienate potential allies or team members who are more pragmatically focused.

- **Overlooking Present Realities:** Your strong future focus can sometimes lead to a disconnect from the current operational needs or the emotional state of your team. The "here and now" might feel mundane or less important compared to the exciting future you envision.

  o *Manifestation:* You might push for a major overhaul without fully appreciating the current workload or anxieties of your team, leading them to feel overwhelmed or unheard. You might also miss crucial details in current projects if your mind is already three steps ahead.

- **Limiting Beliefs:** Common limiting beliefs for a Visionary Maverick might include: "If I can't make it perfect, it's not worth doing," "No one else understands my ideas," or "The details will just bog me down."

Maverick Moves: Tactical Strategies for Thriving

Understanding your strengths and shadows allows you to lead with greater impact. Here are some "Maverick Moves" tailored for you:

1. **Anchor Your Visions with Action Plans:**

   - *Harnessing Strengths:* Continue to dream big and generate those world-changing ideas.
   - *Navigating Shadows:* For every major vision, create a "First Steps" or "Minimum Viable Action" plan. Ask yourself: "What is the smallest possible step I can take today to move this vision forward?" Consider partnering with a Builder or Strategist Maverick who excels at implementation to bring your visions to life.
   - *Tool:* Use a simple "Vision to Action" template: Vision Statement -> Key Milestones -> 3-5 Initial Action Steps (with deadlines and owners).

2. **Cultivate "Visionary Patience" & Inclusive Communication:**

   - *Harnessing Strengths:* Use your gift for articulation to its fullest.
   - *Navigating Shadows:* When communicating your vision, break it down into understandable components. Actively solicit questions and feedback, especially from those who will be involved in implementation. View their questions not as resistance, but as opportunities to clarify and strengthen your plan. Practice active listening.

- *Communication Tip:* Start with the "Why" (the inspiring purpose), then clearly articulate the "What" (the vision itself), and then invite collaboration on the "How" (the implementation).

3. **Bridge the Future with the Present:**

- *Harnessing Strengths:* Your future focus is invaluable.
- *Navigating Shadows:* Dedicate specific time to connect with current realities. Schedule check-ins with your team, focused on present challenges and needs. Ask: "What support do you need *now* to make this future vision possible?" This builds trust and ensures your vision is built on a solid foundation.
- *Self-Care:* Grounding practices like mindfulness, spending time in nature, or engaging in detail-oriented hobbies can help balance your visionary tendencies.

4. **Embrace Imperfect Action Over Inaction:**

- *Navigating Shadows & Limiting Beliefs:* Challenge the belief that your vision must be perfectly executed from day one. Remind yourself that iteration and learning from "imperfect" action are often faster routes to success than waiting for an unattainable perfection.

- *Decision-Making:* When faced with a decision to start something new, if the vision feels aligned and compelling, lean into a "bias for action" for the initial steps, knowing you can refine as you go.

The Visionary Maverick & The Renaissance Themes

Your archetype deeply influences how you engage with the core themes of this book:

- **Redefining Success:** For you, success is often synonymous with actualizing a significant, future-oriented vision. It's less about personal status and more about bringing a groundbreaking idea or transformation into existence.
- **Facing Fear:** Your fears might center on your vision not being understood, not materializing, or being too far ahead of its time. You break through by anchoring into the *power and importance* of your vision.
- **Resilience:** When faced with setbacks, your ability to reconnect with the "why" behind your vision is your greatest source of resilience. You bounce back by re-envisioning the path, not abandoning the destination.
- **Taking Risks:** You are often a natural risk-taker when it comes to pioneering new ideas. Your risks

are usually calculated towards achieving a future possibility that others might deem too audacious.

- **Living from Identity:** Your identity is deeply intertwined with your capacity to see and create what's next. Authenticity for you means honoring and pursuing your unique insights, even when they challenge the status quo.
- **Building Community:** You build community by inviting others into your vision. People are drawn to your clarity and optimism, and you foster connection by uniting them around a shared future purpose.

Affirmations for the Visionary Maverick:

- My vision is clear, powerful, and has the potential to create meaningful change.
- I inspire and uplift others by sharing what I see is possible.
- I embrace the journey from idea to reality with both passion and practical action.
- I trust my ability to see the future and also value the steps needed in the present.
- My bold ideas are needed in the world.

Journal Prompts for Deeper Reflection:

What is one "impossible" vision you hold that, if realized, would bring you profound fulfillment? What is the smallest first step you could take towards it this week?

_____

_____

_____

_____

Think about a time you got stuck in the "idea phase." What was the main obstacle to action, and how might you approach a similar situation differently now?

_____

_____

_____

_____

How can you better communicate your big ideas to those who are more focused on present realities or incremental details, ensuring they feel included and valued?

When your energy for a vision wanes during the implementation phase, what practices or support systems could help you stay engaged and see it through?

A Renaissance Woman Story:
Elara, The Community Garden Dreamer

Elara lived in a dense urban neighborhood with limited green space. Where others saw only concrete and challenges, Elara envisioned a vibrant community garden, a place where residents could connect, grow their own food, and find a pocket of nature. Her vision was expansive: it wasn't just about a few plots; it was about educational workshops, a seed-sharing program, and a small market stand for excess produce.

Initially, her idea was met with skepticism ("Where will we find the space? Who has time? It's too complicated!"). This was the Visionary's classic challenge: her dream felt miles away from current reality. For a while, Elara felt disheartened, her detailed plans gathering dust (a touch of the "castles in the sky" syndrome).

But Elara's belief in her vision was strong. She started small. Instead of trying to build the entire vision at once, she focused on one "Maverick Move". She organized a neighborhood meeting, not to present a finished plan, but to share her dream and ask one question: "What if our neighborhood had a beautiful space where we could all grow together?" She used her strength of inspiring others, painting a picture of children learning about food and elders sharing gardening wisdom.

Her passion was infectious. A few attendees caught the spark. One offered a connection to a city council member about unused land. Another, a retired teacher (a potential Builder Maverick), offered to help organize the practical first steps. Elara, realizing she needed to ground her vision, eagerly collaborated. She learned to listen to pragmatic concerns, adjust timelines, and delegate tasks. It took two years of navigating bureaucracy, fundraising, and community organizing, but Elara's initial "impossible" dream took root. The garden became a reality, not exactly as her first grand vision detailed, but as a thriving, co-created space that transformed her community, all because she dared to see what wasn't there yet and had the courage to take those first, imperfect steps to bring others along.

Illuminating Your Path

Visionary Maverick, your gift is to lift our eyes to the horizon and remind us of what's possible. Your challenge and your growth lie in bridging that beautiful future with the tangible actions of today. By embracing practical steps, collaborating with those who have complementary strengths, and communicating your vision with patience and clarity, you not only dream the future, you actively build it. The world needs your foresight, your optimism, and your unwavering belief in a better tomorrow. Shine on.

CHAPTER 10

The Builder Maverick: Crafting Legacies of Substance

"I don't just want to win, I want to build something that outlives me."
—The Builder Maverick

Welcome, Builder Maverick. You are the architect of endurance, the master of tangible creation. While some are content with fleeting victories, your gaze is fixed on the long term, on constructing something solid, meaningful, and designed to last. You are inherently structured, loyal, and possess a deep-seated focus on legacy. There's a profound satisfaction you derive from the methodical process of creating systems, nurturing growth, and establishing foundations that others can rely upon. You are consistent, intentional, and embody a quiet patience that allows you to see complex projects through to fruition. While you may not always seek the spotlight, your results, the thriving businesses, the strong communities, and well-crafted solutions speak with undeniable volume. You are not flashy; you are foundational, the steady hand that ensures visions become enduring realities.

The Light Side:
Your Signature Strengths in Action

As a Builder Maverick, your strength lies in your methodical and steadfast approach to creating lasting value.

- **Systems Thinking & Process Orientation:** You have an innate ability to see how individual parts connect to form a functional whole. You excel at designing, implementing, and refining systems and processes that create efficiency, predictability, and scalability.
    - *In Action:* A rapidly growing startup is in chaos; information is siloed, and tasks are duplicated. You, the Builder Maverick, step in to design and implement clear operational workflows, communication protocols, and project management systems. Soon, order emerges from the chaos, allowing the team to work more effectively and the business to scale sustainably.
- **Reliability & Consistency:** You are the epitome of dependability. When you commit to something, you see it through with unwavering focus and high standards. Others trust you because your actions are consistent with your words, and your output is predictably excellent.

o *In Action:* In a long-term community project with fluctuating volunteer engagement, you are the constant. You show up week after week, manage the budget meticulously, and ensure core activities continue, providing the stability needed for the project to not only survive but eventually thrive. Your consistency becomes the bedrock others rely on.

- **Focus on Sustainable Growth & Legacy:** You're not interested in quick fixes or short-term gains that compromise long-term stability. Your decisions are guided by a desire for sustainable growth, ensuring that what you build has the strength to endure and serve its purpose for years, even generations, to come.

    o *In Action:* As a financial advisor, you don't push clients towards risky, high-yield investments for a quick win. Instead, you develop comprehensive, long-term financial plans designed for steady, sustainable wealth creation and security, focusing on building a lasting legacy for them and their families.

The Shadow Side:
Potential Pitfalls & "Watch Out For"s

Your dedication to structure and stability can also present challenges if not balanced with flexibility and foresight into different kinds of change.

- **Undervaluing Innovation or Resisting Disruption:** Your comfort with established systems and proven methods can sometimes make you wary of radical innovation or disruptive ideas that threaten the status quo. You might prefer incremental improvements over revolutionary leaps.
  - *Manifestation:* You might be the last to adopt new technologies or methodologies, even if they could offer significant advantages, preferring the "tried and true." In a fast-changing market, this can lead to being outpaced or missing crucial opportunities for growth and evolution.
- **Fear of Disruption & Over-Emphasis on Control:** Because you value order and predictability, unforeseen disruptions or chaotic situations can be particularly challenging. This can lead to an over-emphasis on control, making it difficult to adapt when faced with sudden, unavoidable change.
  - *Manifestation:* You might create overly rigid plans that don't allow for contingencies, or you may struggle to pivot when market conditions shift unexpectedly. This can also make it hard to delegate effectively if you fear others won't maintain your exacting standards or established processes.
- **Potential for Rigidity or Perfectionism:** Your commitment to quality and doing things "the right

way" can sometimes tip into perfectionism or an unwillingness to deviate from the plan, even when circumstances warrant flexibility.

○ *Manifestation:* You might spend excessive time refining details to the point of diminishing returns, or resist creative solutions that don't fit neatly into your existing frameworks. This can slow progress and stifle the very sustainability you aim for if it prevents necessary adaptation.

• **Limiting Beliefs:** Common limiting beliefs for a Builder Maverick might include: "If it ain't broke, don't fix it (even if it's becoming obsolete)," "Big risks are reckless," or "My way is the best way because it's proven."

Maverick Moves:
Tactical Strategies for Thriving

Leverage your building prowess while cultivating adaptability with these strategies:

1. Build in "Innovation Windows":

• *Harnessing Strengths:* Continue to create robust systems and processes.

• *Navigating Shadows:* Intentionally schedule regular "innovation reviews" or "disruption drills" for your projects or organization. Dedicate time to explore new trends, technologies, or alternative approaches. Ask: "If we were to start this today, what might we do differently?" This makes innovation a structured part of your building process.

- *Tool:* Partner with a Visionary or Rebel Maverick for these sessions to bring in fresh, challenging perspectives.

2. Develop "Flexible Frameworks," Not Rigid Rules:

- *Harnessing Strengths:* Your ability to structure is key.
- *Navigating Shadows:* When designing plans and systems, build in contingency plans and allow for adaptability. Think in terms of "flexible frameworks" that guide action but can bend without breaking when faced with unexpected events.
- *Communication Tip:* Clearly communicate the core, non-negotiable elements of a plan, but also identify areas where adaptation and team input are welcome.

3. Embrace "Controlled Experiments" for New Ideas:

- *Harnessing Strengths:* Your methodical nature is perfect for this.

- *Navigating Shadows:* Instead of dismissing a new, disruptive idea outright, approach it as a Builder would: create a small-scale, controlled experiment to test its viability. This allows you to engage with innovation in a structured way, gathering data before committing to a full overhaul.

- *Self-Care:* Recognize that true stability often comes from the ability to adapt. Learning to embrace small, managed changes can reduce the stress associated with larger, unforeseen disruptions.

4. **Delegate with Trust in Process (and People):**

- *Navigating Shadows & Limiting Beliefs:* If you've built strong processes, trust them enough to empower others to execute within them. Combat perfectionism by focusing on "excellent and done" rather than an ever-elusive "perfect."

- *Decision-Making:* When delegating, be clear about outcomes and quality standards but allow room for others to bring their own strengths to the task, even if their *method* slightly differs from yours, as long as the system's integrity is maintained.

The Builder Maverick &
The Renaissance Themes

Your archetype brings a unique perspective to the core Renaissance themes:

- **Redefining Success:** For you, success is tangible and enduring. It's the creation of something valuable that stands the test of time, a well-run company, a strong family foundation, a community institution, a body of work.

- **Facing Fear:** Your fears often relate to instability, chaos, or the potential failure of something you've meticulously built. You overcome fear by reinforcing your foundations, focusing on what you *can* control, and methodically planning for contingencies.

- **Resilience:** Your resilience is rooted in your consistency and your methodical approach. When things break, you don't just patch them; you analyze the failure and rebuild stronger, often with improved systems.

- **Taking Risks:** You approach risks cautiously. You prefer calculated risks where you can see a clear path to a stable outcome. A "bold yes" for you often involves committing to a long-term construction or significant, well-planned expansion rather than a spontaneous leap.

- **Living from Identity:** Your identity is deeply connected to your role as a creator, a stabilizer, and a provider of structure and reliability. You are authentic when you are methodically bringing order and lasting value to the world.
- **Building Community:** You build community by creating safe, stable, and well-organized spaces and structures that people can rely on. You are the one who ensures the community newsletter goes out on time, that the shared resources are well-maintained, or that the group's traditions are honored.

Affirmations for the Builder Maverick:

- I create structures and systems that support lasting success and well-being.
- My consistency and reliability are profound strengths that others trust.
- I build with intention, patience, and a focus on sustainable, meaningful legacies.
- I am open to innovation that enhances the strength and endurance of what I build.
- What I construct has enduring value and makes a tangible difference.

Journal Prompts for Deeper Reflection:

What "legacy" (big or small) are you currently building in your life, work, or community? What makes it meaningful to you?

_____

_____

_____

_____

Reflect on a time you resisted a new idea or change. What was your primary concern? How could you approach a similar situation now with more openness while still honoring your need for stability?

_____

_____

_____

_____

Where might your preference for "doing things the right way" be slowing down progress or preventing necessary adaptation? How can you incorporate more flexibility without sacrificing quality?

_____

_____

_____

_____

Identify one area where you could benefit from a new or improved system. What are the first three steps you could take to design and implement it?

_____

_____

_____

_____

A Renaissance Woman Story: Maria, The Community Health Clinic Founder

Maria, a nurse practitioner, saw a critical gap in healthcare access in her underserved rural community. While others talked about the problem, Maria felt a deep calling to *build* a solution. Her vision wasn't just a clinic; it was a sustainable healthcare hub that would serve generations.

With meticulous planning (a hallmark of the Builder), Maria spent a year researching community needs, navigating grant applications, and developing a comprehensive operational plan. She secured an old, disused building and, with a small team of volunteers, began the painstaking process of renovation. She established clear systems for patient intake, record-keeping, and supply management from day one. Her reliability was legendary; every Tuesday and Thursday, rain or shine, Maria was there, seeing patients, managing the clinic, and training staff.

A few years in, a disruptive force arrived: a well-funded telehealth company offered to "partner" by essentially taking over her patient base with their new app, promising efficiency but threatening the personal, community-centered care Maria had painstakingly built. Her initial reaction was resistance (the Builder's shadow of fearing disruption). The new model felt impersonal and threatened the trusted systems she had established.

However, instead of outright rejecting it, Maria took a "Maverick Move." She conducted a "controlled experiment." She agreed to a small pilot program with a fraction of her patients, carefully integrating the telehealth option for specific services while maintaining her core in-person care. She meticulously tracked outcomes, patient satisfaction, and system impacts. She found that while telehealth couldn't replace the core of her clinic, it *could* enhance certain aspects, like follow-up consultations for stable patients, freeing up in-clinic time for more acute cases. She adapted her systems to incorporate this new tool, not as a replacement, but as an enhancement to the strong foundation she had already built.

Maria's clinic not only survived but expanded its reach, a testament to her ability to build with integrity while strategically embracing innovation to ensure the long-term legacy of her work.

Crafting Your Enduring Impact

Builder Maverick, your capacity to bring order from chaos, to create lasting structures, and to follow through with unwavering consistency is a gift to the world. Your challenge and growth lie in balancing that incredible strength with an openness to evolution and well-considered innovation. By learning to build flexible frameworks, embracing controlled experiments, and trusting the robust systems you create enough to allow for adaptation, you ensure that the legacies you craft are not only strong but also resilient and responsive to the changing world. Your steady hand and far-sighted commitment are what turn fleeting ideas into enduring realities. Continue to build with purpose and patience.

CHAPTER 11

The Disruptor Maverick: Igniting Change and Challenging Norms

"If it makes people uncomfortable, it's probably worth doing."
—The Disruptor Maverick

Welcome, Disruptor Maverick. You are the voice that speaks up when others stay silent, the force that pushes against stagnant norms, the catalyst that ignites necessary change. You're not here to quietly fit in; you're here to flip the table on outdated systems and complacency. With a bold spirit and a sharp mind, you inherently challenge assumptions, question tradition, and courageously say what many are thinking but dare not voice. You are unapologetically different, often seeing the flaws in the status quo with piercing clarity and feeling a deep-seated urgency to provoke evolution. While your approach might make some uncomfortable, it's precisely this discomfort that often sparks the most profound breakthroughs and progress. You are the necessary agitator, the rule-breaker with a purpose, driving us all towards a more honest and evolved future.

The Light Side:
Your Signature Strengths in Action

As a Disruptor Maverick, your power is transformative, pushing boundaries and shaking up ingrained patterns.

- **Speaking Truth to Power & Exposing Incongruities:** You possess a keen ability to see through facades and identify hypocrisy or inefficiency. Crucially, you have the courage to voice these observations, even when it's unpopular or challenges established authority.

  - *In Action:* In a company meeting where a flawed strategy is being presented with unanimous (but hesitant) agreement, you are the one who respectfully but firmly points out the critical inconsistencies and potential negative consequences that everyone else is overlooking, forcing a more honest and productive discussion.

- **Initiating and Championing Change:** You don't just see the need for change; you actively initiate and drive it. You are often at the forefront of new movements, advocating for reforms, or pushing for innovative approaches that can transform an organization or community.

  - *In Action:* Recognizing that your industry has a significant diversity and inclusion problem,

you don't just wait for others to act. You
spearhead an internal task force, develop a
comprehensive proposal with actionable steps,
and tirelessly advocate for its adoption, even in
the face of resistance, ultimately leading to
meaningful policy changes.

- **Courageous Risk-Taking for the Greater Good:**
Your willingness to take risks is often tied to a larger
purpose or a deep conviction about what is right or
necessary. You're not afraid to challenge the status quo,
even if it means facing personal or professional
repercussions, because you believe the potential for
positive impact outweighs the risk.
  - o *In Action:* You see an unethical practice within
    your organization. Despite the potential
    blowback to your career, you choose to
    become a whistleblower or advocate internally
    for corrective action, driven by your
    commitment to integrity and the well-being of
    those affected.

The Shadow Side:
Potential Pitfalls & "Watch Out For"s

Your powerful drive to disrupt can also lead to significant
challenges if not managed with self-awareness and strategic
finesse.

- **Burnout from Always Pushing Boundaries:**
  Constantly being the one to challenge, fight, and push
  against resistance is emotionally and mentally taxing.
  This can lead to chronic stress, exhaustion, and
  eventually, burnout if you don't have strong self-care
  practices and support systems.
  - *Manifestation:* You might find yourself feeling
    perpetually depleted, cynical, or losing the
    passion that initially fueled your disruptive
    efforts. Your physical health might suffer, or
    you may feel isolated in your crusade.
- **Alienating Potential Allies & Misunderstanding
  Your Impact:** Your directness and passion, while
  often necessary, can sometimes be perceived as
  aggressive, overly critical, or dismissive, inadvertently
  alienating people who could otherwise be supporters
  or collaborators. You might be so focused on the
  "what" (the change needed) that the "how" (your
  delivery) creates unintended friction.
  - *Manifestation:* Colleagues might become
    defensive or resistant to your ideas, not
    because the ideas lack merit, but because they
    feel attacked or unheard. You might find
    yourself with fewer allies than you need to
    enact the very changes you seek.
- **Being Perceived as a "Rebel Without a Cause" if
  Vision Isn't Clear:** If your disruptive energy isn't

clearly channeled towards a constructive vision or well-articulated purpose, others might dismiss you as merely contrary or someone who enjoys creating chaos for its own sake, rather than a purposeful change agent.

  o   *Manifestation:* Your valuable critiques might be ignored if people don't understand the positive outcome you're working towards. You might struggle to gain traction for your initiatives because the "why" behind your disruption isn't compellingly communicated.

- **Limiting Beliefs:** Common limiting beliefs for a Disruptor Maverick could be: "It's me against the world," "If I don't fight for it, no one will," "Being liked is less important than being right," or "I have to do this alone."

Maverick Moves:
Tactical Strategies for Thriving

Channel your disruptive power effectively and sustainably with these strategies:

1. Disrupt with Purpose & Strategic Alliances:

Harnessing Strengths: Continue to speak the truth and identify what needs to change.

Navigating Shadows: Before you disrupt, clearly articulate your "why" and the positive vision you're aiming for. Seek out and cultivate relationships with potential allies, Connectors, Builders, or even Visionaries, who can help amplify your message, build bridges, or implement the changes you propose.

Tool: Develop a "Disruption Brief": 1) What's the problem? 2) Why does it matter? 3) What's your proposed solution/vision? 4) Who are the key stakeholders/potential allies?

2. **Practice "Strategic Discomfort" & Empathetic Communication:**

- *Harnessing Strengths:* Your courage to make people uncomfortable is a gift.
- *Navigating Shadows:* Learn to distinguish between necessary discomfort that sparks growth and discomfort that creates unproductive defensiveness. Practice empathetic communication: acknowledge others' perspectives even as you challenge them. Phrase critiques constructively, focusing on the issue or system, not the individuals.
- *Communication Tip:* Use phrases like, "I understand this might be challenging to hear, and my intention is to find a better way forward for all of us..." or "What if we considered this alternative approach to address X concern?"

3. **Prioritize "Sustainable Disruption" & Self-Preservation:**

    *   *Harnessing Strengths:* Your drive is immense.
    *   *Navigating Shadows:* Recognize that you cannot fight every battle, nor can you do it alone. Choose your disruptions strategically, focus on where you can have the most impact. Implement rigorous self-care routines to prevent burnout. Build a strong support system of people who understand and replenish your energy.
    *   *Self-Care:* Schedule regular "off-duty" time where you disengage from your disruptive efforts and focus on activities that recharge you. This is not weakness; it's a strategy for long-term impact.

4. **Pick Your Battles and Know Your Endgame:**

    *   *Navigating Shadows & Limiting Beliefs:* Not every perceived wrong needs your direct intervention. Sometimes, empowering others or working through existing channels can be more effective than direct confrontation. Before engaging, ask yourself: "What is the specific outcome I desire, and is this the most effective way to achieve it?"
    *   *Decision-Making:* Evaluate the potential costs (personal and relational) versus the benefits of a particular disruption. Sometimes, a strategic pause

or a different approach can be more powerful in the long run.

The Disruptor Maverick & The Renaissance Themes (Connecting to Part I)

Your disruptive nature brings a unique fire to the core Renaissance themes:

- **Redefining Success:** For you, success often means dismantling oppressive or outdated systems and creating tangible, equitable change. It's about impact and progress, not just personal gain.
- **Facing Fear:** Your fears might relate to inaction, injustice prevailing, or being silenced. You often face fear head-on, driven by a conviction that is stronger than your apprehension of conflict or criticism.
- **Resilience:** Your resilience is often forged in the fires of opposition. You bounce back from setbacks by re-evaluating your strategy, not your core convictions, and finding new ways to challenge the status quo.
- **Taking Risks:** You are inherently a risk-taker, willing to challenge norms and speak uncomfortable truths even when it's not safe or popular. Your risks are taken in the service of progress.

- **Living from Identity:** Your identity is often that of a truth-teller, a change agent, a voice for the voiceless. Authenticity for you means living in alignment with your core principles of justice, honesty, and progress, even if it makes you an outsider.

- **Building Community:** You might build community among fellow activists or those who share your passion for change. Alternatively, your disruption can sometimes challenge existing community structures, forcing them to become more inclusive or authentic. Your challenge is to build bridges even as you shake foundations.

Affirmations for the Disruptor Maverick:

- My voice is powerful, and I use it to advocate for meaningful change.

- I have the courage to challenge the status quo constructively and fearlessly.

- My disruptive energy, when channeled with purpose, creates positive transformation.

- I can speak the truth *and* build alliances; my impact is stronger with others.

- I prioritize my well-being so I can sustain my efforts for lasting change.

Journal Prompts for Deeper Reflection:

Identify an issue or system you feel a strong urge to disrupt. What is the core truth you want to bring to light? What is the positive vision you hold for what could replace it?

Reflect on a time your disruptive approach alienated someone you wished to influence. How could you have delivered your message differently while maintaining its integrity?

What does "sustainable disruption" look like for you? How can you protect your energy and avoid burnout while still advocating for change?

Who are your potential allies in your current efforts for
change? How can you engage them more effectively?

A Renaissance Woman Story:
Anya, The Corporate Truth-Teller

Anya worked for a large, traditional corporation
where "the way we've always done things" was
practically a company motto. She noticed glaring
inefficiencies and ethically questionable shortcuts in a
major project, practices that were unspoken but widely
tolerated for the sake of expediency. Many colleagues

grumbled privately, but no one spoke up in meetings where senior leadership, including a particularly intimidating VP, lauded the project's "progress."

Anya, a classic Disruptor, felt the incongruity deeply. She knew speaking up carried risks, being labeled a troublemaker, damaging her career prospects, or facing the VP's wrath. For weeks, she wrestled with it, the stress affecting her sleep (a sign of heading towards burnout). She first tried to gather allies, but found most were too fearful to join her publicly.

Finally, in a high-stakes project review, when the VP asked if there were "any final thoughts," Anya took a deep breath. Instead of an aggressive confrontation, she employed a "Maverick Move" by practicing strategic discomfort with empathetic framing. "Thank you for this update," she began, "I appreciate the team's hard work. I do have some questions about the sustainability of X and Y processes, and how they align with our company's stated values of transparency and long-term quality. I'm wondering if we've fully explored alternative approaches that might mitigate some potential future risks I see here?"

Her delivery, though firm, was framed as a question and a concern for the company's own stated values. It made people uncomfortable, yes, but it also opened a tiny crack for honest discussion. The VP was initially defensive, but Anya calmly presented her well-researched points without accusation. While the immediate outcome wasn't a complete overhaul, her courageous act of speaking truth initiated a series of smaller meetings, an internal review, and eventually, significant modifications to the project.

Anya learned that disruption didn't always have to be a full-frontal assault; by strategically choosing her moment and framing her concerns, she could plant seeds of change without completely alienating everyone, though she also made a note to bolster her external support network for future battles.

Igniting Your Impact

Disruptor Maverick, your courage to challenge, question, and provoke is indispensable in a world that too often defaults to complacency. Your path requires immense bravery and a willingness to stand apart. Your growth lies in channeling your powerful, disruptive energy with strategic wisdom, knowing when and how to push, when to build bridges, and always, how to sustain your own fire so you can continue to light the way for necessary evolution. Embrace your role as a catalyst, for it is through Mavericks like you that true progress is ignited.

CHAPTER 12

The Connector Maverick: Weaving Webs of Influence and Belonging

---

"I don't just lead teams, I lead with them."
—The Connector Maverick

Welcome, Connector Maverick. You are the heart of any endeavor, the human bridge who understands that progress and fulfillment are deeply intertwined with meaningful relationships. You possess an innate ability to sense the emotional currents in a room, to understand unspoken needs, and to make individuals feel seen, heard, and valued. Your leadership style is inherently relational and empathetic; you don't just manage people, you lead *through* them and *with* them. Building trust, fostering collaboration, and creating a sense of belonging are not just skills for you; they are a core part of who you are. You know how to read a room better than anyone and can artfully weave together diverse individuals, ideas, and energies to create a cohesive and supportive whole. Your influence often comes not from a formal title but from the genuine care, respect, and understanding you extend to others, making you a natural hub of connection and a powerful, yet often subtle, force for positive collective action.

The Light Side: Your Signature Strengths in Action

As a Connector Maverick, your primary gift lies in your profound understanding and cultivation of human relationships.

- **Emotional Intelligence & Empathy:** You have a high degree of emotional intelligence (EQ), allowing you to perceive, understand, and respond effectively to the emotions of others, as well as your own. Your empathy enables you to genuinely connect with people's experiences and perspectives.
  - o *In Action:* During a tense team meeting where a new project is being met with unspoken resistance, you sense the underlying anxieties. Instead of pushing the agenda, you pause to ask open-ended questions, validate concerns, and create a safe space for team members to voice their worries. This empathetic approach diffuses tension and opens the door for constructive dialogue.
- **Trust-Building & Rapport:** You naturally build trust and rapport with a wide range of people. Your

authenticity, active listening skills, and genuine interest in others make them feel comfortable opening up to you and relying on you.

- o *In Action:* As a new manager joining an established team, you don't immediately impose changes. Instead, you spend time having one-on-one conversations, learning about each team member's strengths, challenges, and aspirations. This investment in understanding builds a strong foundation of trust, making the team more receptive to your leadership and new ideas later on.

- **Fostering Collaboration & Belonging:** You excel at bringing people together, facilitating teamwork, and creating an inclusive environment where everyone feels they belong and can contribute their best. You see the value in diverse perspectives and are skilled at finding common ground.

- o *In Action:* Your organization needs to tackle a complex, cross-departmental challenge. You instinctively identify key individuals from different teams, bring them together, and facilitate a collaborative process that leverages their diverse skills. You ensure every voice is heard and valued, transforming a potentially siloed effort into a synergistic success.

The Shadow Side:
Potential Pitfalls & "Watch Out For"s

Your deep attunement to others and desire for harmony can also present unique challenges if not managed with strong boundaries and self-awareness.

- **Taking on Others' Emotional Labor & Emotional Exhaustion:** Your empathy can lead you to absorb the stress and emotions of those around you. You might become the unofficial 'therapist' or 'confidante' for many, carrying a heavy emotional load that isn't yours, leading to exhaustion and burnout.
    - *Manifestation:* You might find yourself constantly drained after interactions, feeling responsible for everyone's happiness or well-being, and struggling to disconnect from others' problems even in your personal time.
- **Losing Self in Service of Others or Avoiding Conflict:** Your strong desire to maintain relationships and ensure everyone feels good can sometimes lead you to suppress your own needs, opinions, or boundaries. You might avoid necessary conflict or difficult conversations to keep the peace, even if it means sacrificing your own well-being or a better outcome.
    - *Manifestation:* You might consistently say "yes" to requests even when you're overextended, struggle to advocate for your

own career advancement if it feels competitive, or allow your voice to be drowned out in group settings to avoid making waves. This can lead to resentment or a feeling of being undervalued.

- **Difficulty Making Unpopular Decisions:** Because you value relationships and harmony so highly, making decisions that you know will disappoint or upset some people can be incredibly difficult, even if those decisions are necessary for the greater good of the team or organization.

  o *Manifestation:* You might procrastinate on tough decisions, try to please everyone (which is often impossible), or water down a necessary change to the point where it loses its effectiveness, all to avoid relational discomfort.

- **Limiting Beliefs:** Common limiting beliefs for a Connector Maverick might include: "It's my job to make everyone happy," "If I assert my needs, I'll damage the relationship," "Conflict is always bad," or "My worth is tied to how much others like or need me."

Maverick Moves: Tactical Strategies for Thriving

Channel your connecting super-powers effectively while protecting your own energy and voice:

1. **Practice "Empathetic Detachment" & Set Energetic Boundaries:**

    - *Harnessing Strengths:* Continue to be empathetic and attuned to others.
    - *Navigating Shadows:* Learn to offer support and understanding without taking on others' emotions as your own. Visualize an "energetic shield" or practice mindfulness to create a healthy separation. Clearly define what emotional support you can offer and for how long.
    - *Tool:* Develop go-to phrases like, "I can hear this is really challenging for you, and I support you in finding a solution. What steps are you considering?" (This shows care without taking ownership of solving their problem).

2. **Prioritize Your Needs & Voice with "Relational Courage":**

    - *Harnessing Strengths:* Your understanding of relationships is an asset here.
    - *Navigating Shadows:* Recognize that true connection thrives on authenticity, which includes expressing your own needs and perspectives. Practice "relational courage" – the bravery to have honest, respectful conversations even when they are uncomfortable. Reframe conflict as an

opportunity for deeper understanding and stronger relationships when handled constructively.

- *Communication Tip:* Use "I" statements to express your needs: "I need some time to focus on this project right now," or "I feel concerned when X happens, and I'd like to discuss how we can approach it differently."

3. **Build "Consensus with Conviction" for Decision-Making:**

- *Harnessing Strengths:* Your ability to bring people together is key.
- *Navigating Shadows:* When facing tough decisions, involve others in the process and gather diverse input (consensus-building). However, once a decision is made (especially if it's yours to make), communicate it with clarity and conviction, explaining the rationale, even if it's not universally popular. Acknowledge the impact on others while standing firm in the necessary direction.
- *Self-Care:* Recognize that you cannot please everyone. Your role is to make the best decision possible for the collective, and that sometimes involves navigating temporary discomfort for long-term health.

4. **Schedule "Connection Time" and "Recharge Time" Intentionally:**

    - *Harnessing Strengths & Navigating Shadows:* Your energy is deeply affected by your interactions. Be as intentional about scheduling time for meaningful connections that energize you as you are about scheduling solitary "recharge time" to process emotions and replenish your own well-being, especially after intense interpersonal engagements.
    - *Decision-Making:* Before committing to social or professional engagements, check in with your own energy levels. It's okay to decline an invitation if you're feeling depleted.

The Connector Maverick & The Renaissance Themes

Your connecting abilities profoundly shape your engagement with the core Renaissance themes:

- **Redefining Success:** For you, success is often measured by the quality of your relationships, the strength of the teams you build, and the positive impact you have on the people around you. A thriving network and a sense of belonging are key indicators.
- **Facing Fear:** Your fears may revolve around relational conflict, disappointing others, loneliness,

or social rejection. You overcome these fears by leaning into your ability to build bridges, communicate empathetically, and seek mutually supportive solutions.

- **Resilience:** Your resilience is often found in your support network. When you face setbacks, you draw strength from trusted relationships and your ability to rally collective support. You also help others be resilient through your empathetic presence.
- **Taking Risks:** You might be cautious about risks that could damage key relationships. However, you will take significant "relational risks," like mediating a high-stakes conflict or vouching for someone, when you believe it can lead to greater harmony or a stronger community.
- **Living from Identity:** Your identity is deeply rooted in your role as a facilitator of connection, a builder of community, and an empathetic presence. You are most authentic when you are nurturing relationships and fostering a sense of belonging.
- **Building Community:** This is your superpower. You don't just participate in communities; you actively weave them, strengthen them, and ensure they are inclusive and supportive environments where people feel they truly belong.

Affirmations for the Connector Maverick:

- My ability to connect with and understand others is a profound strength.
- I build strong, authentic relationships that foster trust and collaboration.
- I can be empathetic and supportive while maintaining healthy boundaries.
- My voice and needs are important, and I express them with relational courage.
- I create spaces where people feel seen, valued, and connected.

Journal Prompts for Deeper Reflection:

Think about the relationships that energize you the most. What qualities make these connections so fulfilling? How can you cultivate more of these?

When was the last time you avoided a difficult conversation to keep the peace? What was the outcome? If you could go back, how might you approach it with "relational courage"?

_____

_____

_____

_____

In what situations do you find yourself taking on too much emotional labor for others? What's one boundary you can set this week to protect your energy?

_____

_____

_____

_____

How can you leverage your connecting skills to bring people together around a shared purpose or to solve a particular challenge in your work or community?

_____

A Renaissance Woman Story: Lena, The Team Unifier

Lena was a project manager in a tech company known for its brilliant but often siloed engineers. A critical new product was falling behind schedule due to poor communication and simmering tensions between the hardware and software teams. Deadlines were being missed, blame was being tossed around, and morale was plummeting.

Lena, a natural Connector Maverick, sensed the deep frustration and lack of trust. Instead of just imposing new deadlines or processes, she started by having individual, informal coffee chats with key members of both teams. She didn't try to solve the technical problems; she listened, truly listened, to their frustrations, their perspectives on the challenges, and what they needed to feel supported. She learned that the hardware team felt the software team didn't understand their constraints, and the software team felt the hardware team was too rigid.

Armed with this understanding, Lena organized a carefully facilitated off-site meeting. She didn't call it a "problem-solving session" but a "Team Connection and Re-alignment Day." She started with activities designed to help team members see each other as people first, sharing personal work styles and communication preferences. Then, she guided them through a structured but empathetic discussion about the project's pain points, ensuring everyone had a voice and that concerns were validated without blame. She masterfully highlighted their shared goal, a successful product launch, and helped them co-create new communication protocols and shared problem-solving approaches.

There were moments of discomfort, but Lena's calm, empathetic facilitation kept the conversation constructive. By the end of the day, the atmosphere had shifted palpably. The teams weren't just agreeing on a new plan; they were talking, laughing, and seeing each other as allies rather than adversaries. Lena knew this was just the beginning; she followed up by establishing regular cross-team check-ins and informal social gatherings. The project got back on track, not just because of a new plan, but because Lena had re-woven the human fabric of the team, replacing distrust with understanding and a shared sense of purpose. She didn't just manage the project; she led the people.

Weaving Your Web of Impact

Connector Maverick, your ability to foster genuine connection, build trust, and create inclusive environments is not a "soft skill," it is a profound leadership strength, essential for any thriving endeavor. Your challenge and growth lie in extending that same empathy and care to yourself by honoring your own needs, setting healthy boundaries, and using your voice with courage even when it risks temporary discomfort. When you master this balance, your capacity to weave together people and ideas for collective success becomes an unstoppable force for good. The world desperately needs your heart, your empathy, and your unique gift for reminding us that we are, indeed, stronger together.

CHAPTER 13

The Strategist Maverick: Architecting Success with Precision and Foresight

---

"I don't need to be loud to be effective. I move when it matters."

—The Strategist Maverick

Welcome, Strategist Maverick. You are the master planner, the analytical mind that sees the chessboard of life and work with exceptional clarity, always thinking ten steps ahead. Your power is not in volume but in precision; you are calculating, intentional, and quietly formidable. While others may be caught up in reacting to immediate events, you are already deconstructing complex situations, identifying underlying patterns, and meticulously building the roadmap towards a desired outcome. You don't necessarily seek the spotlight, finding deeper satisfaction in the intellectual rigor of analysis, the elegance of a well-crafted plan, and the flawless execution of a strategy. Others depend on your foresight, your ability to solve intricate problems, and your capacity for decisive action when the moment is right. You are the architect of success, building pathways with deliberate thought and impactful moves.

The Light Side:
Your Signature Strengths in Action

As a Strategist Maverick, your core strengths lie in your analytical capabilities and your gift for effective planning and execution.

- **Exceptional Problem-Solving:** You have a keen ability to dissect complex problems into manageable components, analyze them from multiple angles, and develop innovative and effective solutions. You see connections and root causes that others might miss.
  - o *In Action:* An organization faces a recurring, costly issue that baffles other leaders. You dive deep into the data, interview key personnel, and map out the entire process, ultimately identifying a hidden bottleneck and a series of interconnected systemic flaws. You then propose a multi-pronged solution that not only solves the immediate problem but also prevents future recurrences.
- **Pattern Recognition & Foresight:** You are adept at identifying trends, patterns, and potential future scenarios based on current data and subtle cues. This allows you to anticipate challenges and opportunities,

positioning yourself and your endeavors for optimal outcomes.

- o *In Action:* Observing subtle shifts in consumer behavior and emerging technologies within your industry, you accurately predict a significant market disruption. You then develop a proactive strategy for your company to adapt its offerings and business model, allowing it to not only weather the change but also to emerge as a leader in the new landscape.

- **Decisive Action & Precision Execution:** While you are thorough in your analysis, you are not afraid to take decisive action once a strategy is formulated. You move with intention and precision, ensuring that plans are executed efficiently and effectively to achieve the desired results.

- o *In Action:* After a period of careful planning for a new product launch, you identify the optimal market window. You then orchestrate the launch with meticulous attention to detail, coordinating all moving parts, marketing, sales, and operations, to ensure a seamless and impactful rollout, hitting all key metrics precisely as planned.

The Shadow Side:
Potential Pitfalls & "Watch Out For"s

Your powerful intellect and desire for precision can also lead to certain challenges if not consciously managed.

- **Overthinking & Analysis Paralysis:** Your ability to see all angles and potential pitfalls can sometimes lead to getting stuck in analysis, endlessly weighing options, and gathering more data without moving to a decision. The desire for the "perfect" strategy can delay necessary action.
  - *Manifestation:* You might find yourself spending weeks or months refining a plan, missing crucial windows of opportunity, or frustrating team members who are waiting for direction. You may also experience significant internal stress from the constant mental churn.
- **Perfectionism & Intolerance for Error:** Your high standards for yourself and your work can sometimes manifest as unforgiving perfectionism. This can make it difficult to delegate, lead to micromanaging tendencies, or create an environment where others are afraid to make mistakes.
  - *Manifestation:* You might redo work done by others if it doesn't meet your exacting standards, struggle with "good enough" solutions even when they are practical, or

inadvertently stifle creativity and initiative in your team due to an implicit expectation of flawlessness.

- **Appearing Detached or Overly Critical:** Your intense focus on logic, data, and strategy can sometimes lead to you being perceived as emotionally detached, overly critical, or dismissive of the more human, intuitive, or relational aspects of a situation.
  - o *Manifestation:* Team members might feel that their contributions are only valued if they are purely data-driven, or they might find your feedback overly harsh if it's not balanced with acknowledgment of effort or relational context. This can impact team morale and open communication.
- **Limiting Beliefs:** Common limiting beliefs for a Strategist Maverick could be: "I must have all the information before I can act," "Mistakes are unacceptable," "If I don't control every detail, it will fail," or "Feelings are irrelevant in decision-making."

Maverick Moves:
Tactical Strategies for Thriving

Maximize your strategic brilliance while fostering agility and connection with these approaches:

1. **Set "Action Thresholds" for Analysis:**

   - *Harnessing Strengths:* Continue your thorough analysis and planning.
   - *Navigating Shadows:* To combat analysis paralysis, define clear "action thresholds" for decision-making. For example: "Once I have 70-80% of the information and have considered the top 3 risks, I will make a decision and move forward." Or, set time limits for the analysis phase of a project.
   - *Tool:* Use a "Decision Matrix" to objectively weigh options based on pre-defined criteria, which can help accelerate the move from analysis to choice.

2. **Embrace "Strategic Imperfection" & Iteration:**

   - *Harnessing Strengths:* Your high standards are valuable.
   - *Navigating Shadows:* Reframe perfectionism by embracing the concept of "strategic imperfection" or "iterative excellence." Launch a well-thought-out version 1.0 of a plan or product, gather real-world feedback, and then iterate and improve. This allows for learning and adaptation, which is often more effective than striving for elusive upfront perfection.
   - *Communication Tip:* When delegating, clearly define the "critical success factors" and "acceptable

quality standards," empowering your team to deliver effectively without needing to replicate your exact thought process for every minor detail.

3. **Integrate "Human Data" with Analytical Data:**

- *Harnessing Strengths:* Your analytical skills are top-notch.
- *Navigating Shadows:* Make a conscious effort to seek out and value "human data," team morale, stakeholder emotions, and intuitive insights from trusted colleagues (especially Connectors or Alchemists). Schedule time to actively listen and understand these perspectives.
- *Self-Care:* Recognize that factoring in the human element doesn't dilute your strategy; it often strengthens it by improving buy-in, identifying unforeseen human-related risks, and fostering a more supportive environment.

4. **Communicate the "Why" Behind the "What":**

- *Navigating Shadows & Limiting Beliefs:* When presenting your strategies or decisions, don't just lay out the logical "what." Take the time to explain the "why," the overarching goals, the patterns you observed, and the potential benefits. This helps others understand your thinking and feel more engaged, rather than just being handed a directive.

- *Decision-Making:* Involve trusted team members in *parts* of the strategic thinking process where appropriate. This not only provides them with context but can also enrich your analysis with diverse perspectives.

The Strategist Maverick & The Renaissance Themes

Your strategic mind interacts with the core Renaissance themes in a distinct way:

- **Redefining Success:** For you, success is often the elegant and effective execution of a well-designed plan that achieves a significant, often complex, objective. It's the intellectual satisfaction of a problem solved masterfully.
- **Facing Fear:** Your fears may center on unforeseen variables disrupting your plans, making a miscalculation, or the chaos of an unmanaged situation. You combat fear with meticulous planning, risk assessment, and developing contingency strategies.
- **Resilience:** Your resilience comes from your ability to analyze setbacks objectively, learn from what went wrong, and then recalibrate your strategy to overcome the obstacle. You don't dwell on failure; you dissect it for data.

- **Taking Risks:** You are not typically a spontaneous risk-taker. Your risks are calculated, assessed, and mitigated as much as possible. A "bold yes" for you is often the culmination of deep analysis leading to a high-stakes, strategic move.

- **Living from Identity:** Your identity is deeply connected to your intellect, your competence, and your ability to bring order and effective solutions to complex challenges. Authenticity for you is about applying your strategic mind with integrity and purpose.

- **Building Community:** You might build community by creating effective team structures, developing clear roles and responsibilities that allow groups to function optimally, or by providing the strategic framework that enables a collective to achieve its goals. You contribute through clarity and well-thought-out plans.

Affirmations for the Strategist Maverick:

- My analytical mind is a powerful asset for creating clarity and effective solutions.
- I make well-reasoned decisions and execute plans with precision and foresight.
- I trust my ability to see patterns and anticipate future needs effectively.

- I balance thorough analysis with timely, decisive action.
- My strategic contributions create a significant and lasting impact.

Journal Prompts for Deeper Reflection:

Describe a complex problem you successfully solved. What specific strategic thinking skills did you employ? How can you apply those more consistently?

When do you most often find yourself falling into "analysis paralysis" or perfectionism? What is one "action threshold" or "good enough" principle you can implement?

How can you more intentionally incorporate "human data" or relational considerations into your strategic planning without feeling it compromises your analytical rigor?

_____

_____

_____

_____

Think of a current goal. What's the overarching strategy, and what are the first 3-5 precise, actionable steps you can take to move it forward?

_____

_____

_____

_____

A Renaissance Woman Story:
Isabella, The Turnaround CEO

Isabella was appointed CEO of a legacy company that was rapidly losing market share to newer, more agile competitors. The company was riddled with inefficiencies, outdated technology, and a culture resistant to change. Morale was low, and the board was looking for a miracle.

Isabella, a quintessential Strategist Maverick, didn't panic. She spent her first ninety days in deep analysis mode. She immersed herself in financial reports, operational data, market research, and conducted discreet interviews across all levels of the company. She didn't make any immediate, flashy announcements. Instead, she quietly pieced together a complex puzzle, identifying core strengths that were being underutilized, critical weaknesses that were being ignored, and emerging market opportunities that the company was blind to. This initial phase of intense, quiet analysis was crucial; some observers mistook her silence for inaction (a common misinterpretation of the Strategist's "Watch Out For" of appearing detached while actually deep in thought).

After three months, Isabella presented her comprehensive turnaround strategy to the board. It was a masterclass in precision: a multi-year plan with clear phases, specific departmental objectives, measurable KPIs, identified risks, and detailed contingency plans. It wasn't just a vision; it was a meticulously constructed roadmap. She addressed the need for technological upgrades, process re-engineering, and a difficult but necessary restructuring.

The "perfectionism" shadow appeared when some departments pushed back on the speed or specifics of certain changes. Isabella's initial instinct was to rigidly enforce the plan. However, remembering the importance of buy-in (a "Maverick Move" to integrate human data), she scheduled focused sessions with resistant teams, not to abandon her strategy, but to explain the "why" behind specific decisions and to listen to their operational insights, making minor tactical adjustments where feasible without compromising the core strategy. This slightly iterative approach, blending her precise plan with stakeholder input, increased engagement. Within two years, the company had stabilized, regained market share, and was innovating again—all because Isabella had the foresight to analyze deeply, the courage to plan boldly, and the precision to execute effectively, while learning to temper her plan with strategic engagement.

Architecting Your Impact

Strategist Maverick, your ability to think critically, plan with foresight, and act with precision is an invaluable asset in a world often starved for clarity and effective execution. Your challenge and growth lie in balancing your analytical rigor with timely action, your high standards with an appreciation for iterative progress, and your logical focus with an understanding of the human element. When you harness your strategic mind in this holistic way, you don't just devise plans; you architect impactful realities. Trust your intellect, value your precision, and continue to move when it truly matters. The world needs your quiet power to build a more effective and intentional future.

CHAPTER 14

The Rebel Maverick: Igniting Action with Instinct and Audacity

"I leap first. And then I figure it out."
—The Rebel Maverick

Welcome, Rebel Maverick. You are the embodiment of audacious action, the one who trusts her gut implicitly and moves with a speed and confidence that can be breathtaking. You are inherently intuitive, bold, and possess a natural inclination to break through boundaries that seem to confine others. While some wait for permission or a perfectly laid-out plan, you operate on instinct, speaking freely, acting swiftly, and often shaking up the spaces you inhabit simply by being your unapologetic self. Your brilliance often lies in your bravery, your willingness to take the leap, to challenge conventions not by meticulously dismantling them, but by audaciously disregarding them in pursuit of a goal or a deeply felt truth. You don't just think outside the box; you often act as if the box doesn't even exist, inspiring others through your fearless pursuit of what feels right and true in the moment.

The Light Side:
Your Signature Strengths in Action

As a Rebel Maverick, your power lies in your swift, instinct-driven engagement with the world.

- **Quick, Decisive Action:** You have an unparalleled ability to assess a situation rapidly and take decisive action. You don't get bogged down in over-analysis; when your intuition signals "go," you move. This allows you to seize opportunities that others might miss while they're still deliberating.
  - *In Action:* A sudden market opportunity appears with a very short window. While other teams are scheduling meetings to discuss strategy, you've already initiated contact, pitched a preliminary idea based on your gut feeling, and secured a tentative agreement, putting your team miles ahead.

- **Instinctual Leadership & Gut-Driven Decisions:** You possess a strong inner compass and a deep trust in your intuition. You often "just know" the right course of action, even if you can't immediately articulate all the logical reasons why. This instinctual clarity can be a powerful guiding force for yourself and those who trust your leadership.
  - *In Action:* When faced with a complex hiring decision between two equally qualified

candidates, you choose the one your gut strongly favors, even if their resume is slightly less conventional. This candidate later proves to be an exceptional fit, bringing a unique perspective that transforms the team's dynamic for the better.

- **Unshakeable Confidence & Fearlessness:** You exude a natural confidence that allows you to take bold steps and break boundaries without excessive hand-wringing. Your inherent bravery inspires those around you and can make seemingly impossible feats achievable.
  - o *In Action:* Your team is daunted by a new, highly ambitious project that no one else in the industry has successfully tackled. Your unwavering belief that "we can do this" and your willingness to dive in headfirst, tackling the first obstacles with fearless energy, galvanizes the team and transforms their doubt into determination.

The Shadow Side:
Potential Pitfalls & "Watch Out For"s

Your incredible speed and audacity, if not tempered with some foresight and consideration for consequences, can lead to challenges.

- **Impulsivity & Unforeseen Consequences:** Your "leap first, figure it out later" approach, while often a strength, can sometimes result in impulsive decisions made without fully considering the downstream consequences for yourself or others. This can lead to cleaning up messes or navigating unintended negative impacts.

  o *Manifestation:* You might launch a new initiative with great enthusiasm but without adequate planning for resources or stakeholder buy-in, leading to it fizzling out or creating conflict. Or, you might speak a blunt truth in a sensitive situation without considering the relational fallout.

- **Struggling with Follow-Through & Sustained Effort:** The thrill for you is often in the initiation, the bold leap, the breaking of new ground. Once the initial excitement wanes or a project requires long-term, detailed, and consistent effort, you might lose interest or struggle to maintain focus, moving on to the next "rebellious" act.

  o *Manifestation:* You might have a string of brilliantly started but unfinished projects. Team members might feel whiplash from your shifting priorities or frustrated by a lack of sustained support for initiatives you championed.

- **Disregard for Necessary Rules or Structures:** While your ability to bypass bureaucracy can be an asset, a wholesale disregard for all rules or established structures can sometimes create chaos, alienate those who value order (like Builder Mavericks), or lead to unnecessary risks if important protocols are ignored.
  - *Manifestation:* You might skip crucial steps in a process to save time, only to find it creates bigger problems later. Or, your tendency to "do it your way" might clash with organizational policies or team agreements, leading to friction.
- **Limiting Beliefs:** Common limiting beliefs for a Rebel Maverick might include: "Rules are for other people," "Planning just slows me down," "If it's not exciting, it's not worth doing," or "Cleaning up the details is someone else's job."

Maverick Moves: Tactical Strategies for Thriving

Channel your rebellious spirit into potent and sustainable action with these strategies:

1. Pair Your Leap with a "Quick Scan":

- *Harnessing Strengths:* Keep trusting your gut and your ability to act fast.

- *Navigating Shadows:* Before you leap, train yourself to do a 60-second "consequence scan." Ask: "What's the best-case scenario? What's a likely worst-case scenario? Who else will this impact?" This doesn't mean paralysis by analysis, just a moment of rapid foresight to mitigate impulsive blind spots.
- *Tool:* For bigger leaps, quickly identify one "anchor point," a trusted advisor (perhaps a Strategist) or a single, critical success factor to keep in mind as you move.

2. **Find Your "Follow-Through Partner" or System:**

- *Harnessing Strengths:* Your strength is initiation; leverage that.
- *Navigating Shadows:* Acknowledge that long-term follow-through might not be your favorite part. Partner with someone who excels at details and completion (like a Builder Maverick). Alternatively, create simple, motivating systems for yourself, like breaking down long projects into smaller, rebellious "sprints" with exciting mini-goals.
- *Communication Tip:* When starting something new, be upfront with your team: "I'm fantastic at getting this off the ground with a bang. I'll need

[Name/Type of Support] to help carry it through the detailed phases."

3. **Learn "Strategic Rule-Bending" vs. Reckless Rule-Breaking:**

- *Harnessing Strengths:* Your willingness to challenge norms is vital.
- *Navigating Shadows:* Understand which rules are truly arbitrary and stifling, and which ones exist for crucial safety, ethical, or legal reasons. If a rule needs to be broken for progress, do it with awareness and a clear "why," rather than just for the thrill of rebellion.
- *Self-Care:* Recognize that not all structures are prisons. Some can provide a necessary container for your energy, preventing burnout and ensuring your rebellious acts have a more focused and lasting impact.

4. **Communicate Your "Intuitive Hits" with a Dash of Context:**

- *Harnessing Strengths & Navigating Shadows:* When your gut tells you to move, and you need others on board, take a brief moment to articulate any fragments of the "why" that you *can* perceive. Even a short explanation like, "My instinct is telling me we need to pivot hard on this, and here's

the one key reason I feel it so strongly right now..."
can help others trust your leap, rather than just
seeing it as purely impulsive.

- *Decision-Making:* Trust your gut, but also value
  the data that can quickly validate (or caution
  against) an intuitive hit, especially when the stakes
  are high.

The Rebel Maverick & The Renaissance Themes

Your rebellious streak infuses the core Renaissance themes
with dynamic energy:

- **Redefining Success:** For you, success is often
  about freedom, authenticity, and the thrill of
  breaking new ground or proving a bold idea can
  work. It's less about conventional accolades and
  more about living life on your own terms, fully
  expressed.

- **Facing Fear:** While you appear fearless, your
  "fear" might be more about being constrained,
  bored, or inauthentic. You combat this by taking
  action, trusting your impulses, and breaking free
  from what feels stifling.

- **Resilience:** Your resilience is often demonstrated
  by your ability to bounce back quickly from
  setbacks, shake off failures as learning experiences,

and dive into the next challenge with renewed enthusiasm. You don't dwell; you act.

- **Taking Risks:** You are arguably the most natural risk-taker among the archetypes, often thriving on the adrenaline of uncertainty and the challenge of navigating uncharted territory. Your risks are bold and often intuitive.

- **Living from Identity:** Your identity is deeply tied to your freedom, your boldness, and your authenticity. You are most yourself when you are unconstrained, speaking your truth, and acting in direct alignment with your gut feelings.

- **Building Community:** You might build community with other non-conformists or by inspiring a group to take a collective leap of faith. You attract those drawn to your energy and courage, though your independent streak means you also need space.

Affirmations for the Rebel Maverick:

- My intuition is a powerful guide, and I trust its wisdom.
- I have the courage to act decisively and break through unnecessary barriers.
- My boldness inspires action and opens up new possibilities.

- I can be both a powerful initiator and a committed finisher when I choose.
- I embrace my authentic self fearlessly and live life on my own terms.

Journal Prompts for Deeper Reflection:

Recall a time you took a significant leap based purely on your intuition. What was the outcome, and what did it teach you about trusting your gut?

_____

_____

_____

_____

When does your need for quick action or your dislike of constraints tend to get you into trouble? What's one "quick scan" or "anchor point" strategy you could try next time?

_____

_____

_____

_____

Who in your life could be a good "follow-through partner" for your brilliant ideas? How could you enlist their support in a way that honors both your strengths?

_____

_____

_____

_____

What "rule" (societal, professional, or self-imposed) feels most stifling to you right now? What would one small act of "strategic rebellion" against it look like?

_____

_____

_____

_____

A Renaissance Woman Story:
Chloe, The Unconventional Fundraiser

Chloe was tasked with fundraising for a small, innovative arts non-profit that was struggling for visibility against larger, more established institutions. The traditional fundraising methods, gala dinners, lengthy grant applications, and corporate sponsorships, were yielding minimal results and felt soul-crushingly slow to her.

Chloe, a Rebel Maverick through and through, felt her gut screaming for a different approach. While her board (comprised of well-meaning Builder and Strategist types) urged caution and adherence to proven models, Chloe had an intuitive hit: a pop-up, immersive art experience in an unexpected, gritty urban location, with a "pay-what-you-can-if-you-love-it" model, culminating in a raucous, art-fueled party to attract younger donors. It was a huge departure from their norm.

Her "leap first" instinct kicked in. Before getting full formal approval, she used her confidence to secure a temporary, near-free space and rallied a few artist friends to mock up a concept. This quick action created tangible excitement. However, her impulsivity initially overlooked key logistical details and the need for board buy-in for the financial model (her shadow of struggling with follow-through on the "boring" parts).

When the board raised concerns about financial viability and potential chaos, Chloe, instead of digging in her heels, employed a "Maverick Move." She quickly brought in a volunteer (a Connector with Builder tendencies) to help her map out a basic budget, a security plan, and a clear communication strategy for the board, addressing their concerns while protecting the rebellious core of her idea. She didn't let the planning slow her momentum but used it to channel her energy more effectively.

The event was a wild, unconventional success. It generated buzz, attracted a new demographic of supporters, and raised more seed money through passionate, small donations than their previous, stuffy gala. Chloe learned that her rebellious instincts were powerful, but pairing them with a modicum of strategic planning and enlisting help for the details made her impact even more profound and sustainable.

Igniting Your Audacious Path

Rebel Maverick, your fearless energy, your intuitive leaps, and your refusal to be boxed in are vital sparks in a world that often errs on the side of caution. You show us what's possible when we dare to act on our deepest instincts. Your growth lies in learning to harness that incredible power with a touch of foresight and a commitment to seeing your most brilliant rebellions through to their full impact. Find trusted partners for the details, do a quick scan before you leap into the unknown, and never lose that audacious spirit. The world needs your courage to break open new paths and ignite action. Leap on.

CHAPTER 15

The Alchemist Maverick: Transforming Challenges into Purpose and Wisdom

---

"My growth didn't come easy, but it came sacred." —The Alchemist Maverick

---

Welcome, Alchemist Maverick. You are the soulful transformer, the one who possesses the rare and profound ability to turn pain into purpose, adversity into wisdom, and lead from a place of deep grace and understanding. You feel things with an extraordinary depth, and this emotional richness, rather than being a burden, becomes a source of profound insight and intuitive guidance. You are inherently purpose-driven, grounded in meaning, and often feel a calling to heal, elevate, or bring restoration to the spaces and people you touch. Your journey may not have been easy, but every challenge has been a crucible, forging a resilient spirit and an ability to see the sacred in the struggle. You don't just navigate difficulties; you transmute them, emerging with lessons that not only empower you but also illuminate the path for others.

The Light Side:
Your Signature Strengths in Action

As an Alchemist Maverick, your unique power lies in your capacity for deep transformation and your ability to guide others through their own.

- **Meaning-Making & Purpose-Finding:** You have an exceptional ability to find meaning and purpose even in the most challenging circumstances. You can reframe adversity as an opportunity for growth and help others see the lessons and potential for transformation within their own struggles.
    - *In Action:* After a significant organizational crisis or personal setback that leaves many feeling lost and demoralized, you are the one who helps the collective process the experience, extract valuable lessons, and find a renewed sense of purpose and direction, guiding them from despair to a place of hope and learning.
- **Emotional Depth & Intuitive Wisdom:** Your capacity to feel deeply gives you profound access to emotional intelligence and intuitive wisdom. You understand the unspoken currents of human experience and can connect with others on a soul level, offering insights that resonate with deep truth.

o *In Action:* When a team member is struggling with a personal issue that's impacting their work, you don't just address the performance; you sense the underlying emotional distress. With compassion and intuitive guidance, you create a space for them to feel understood, offering support or resources that address the root cause, fostering loyalty and well-being.

- **Transformative Resilience & Healing Presence:** You have not only endured hardship but have learned to transmute it into strength and wisdom. This gives you a potent resilience and a calming, healing presence that can help others navigate their own difficult times and find their own capacity for healing and growth.

  o *In Action:* In a community reeling from loss or a difficult change, your grounded presence and ability to hold space for grief while gently pointing towards hope and rebuilding becomes a source of comfort and strength. You facilitate processes that allow for collective healing and the emergence of a stronger, more connected group.

The Shadow Side:
Potential Pitfalls & "Watch Out For"s

Your profound empathy and dedication to healing can also lead to vulnerability if not managed with strong self-awareness and boundaries.

- **Emotional Exhaustion & Vicarious Traumatization:** Your deep attunement to the suffering of others means you can easily absorb their pain and emotional burdens. Without diligent, energetic hygiene, this can lead to profound emotional exhaustion, compassion fatigue, or even vicarious traumatization.
  - *Manifestation:* You might find yourself constantly feeling drained, overwhelmed by the weight of the world, or experiencing symptoms of burnout directly related to your empathetic engagement with others' hardships. Sleep disturbances or a persistent sense of sadness can occur.
- **Overextending for Others & Porous Boundaries:** Your innate desire to help and heal can lead you to consistently overextend yourself, putting others' needs far ahead of your own. This can result in porous personal and professional boundaries, making it difficult to say "no" even when you are depleted.
  - *Manifestation:* You might be the go-to person for everyone's problems, finding your own work and well-being constantly interrupted or sacrificed. This can lead to resentment, physical illness, or a loss of your own creative energy as you become a container for everyone else.

- **Difficulty Disengaging or Becoming Over-Involved:** Because you feel things so deeply and are committed to transformation, you may find it hard to disengage from situations or people you are trying to help, even when it's healthy or necessary to do so. You might become overly invested in others' outcomes.
  - ○ *Manifestation:* You might struggle to let go of a mentoring relationship that has run its course, or you might continue to pour energy into a dysfunctional system, hoping to "fix" it, long after it's clear that your efforts are not yielding results or are actively harming you.
- **Limiting Beliefs:** Common limiting beliefs for an Alchemist Maverick might include: "It's my responsibility to heal everyone's pain," "My worth comes from how much I can help others," "If I don't take on their burden, who will?" or "Prioritizing my own needs is selfish."

Maverick Moves:
Tactical Strategies for Thriving

Sustain your transformative gifts by integrating these protective and empowering practices:

1. **Practice "Sacred Self-Preservation" & Energetic Cleansing:**

   - *Harnessing Strengths:* Your ability to transform extends to yourself.

- *Navigating Shadows:* Develop non-negotiable self-care rituals specifically focused on emotional and energetic cleansing. This could include mindfulness, meditation, spending time in nature, journaling, physical activity, or creative expression. Actively visualize releasing any absorbed energy that is not yours.

- *Tool:* Create a "Transition Ritual" after intense helping encounters, a few minutes of deep breathing, washing your hands with intention, or listening to calming music to consciously disconnect and recenter.

2. **Establish "Compassionate Boundaries" with Clarity & Grace:**

- *Harnessing Strengths:* Use your emotional intelligence to communicate boundaries kindly but firmly.

- *Navigating Shadows:* Recognize that strong boundaries are not a rejection of others, but an act of self-love and sustainability. Practice saying "no" gracefully when you are at capacity. Clearly define the scope and limits of the support you can offer.

- *Communication Tip:* "I deeply empathize with what you're going through. While I can offer [specific, limited support, e.g., 'a listening ear for 30 minutes' or 'this resource'], I also need to honor my own capacity right now so I can continue to be present."

3. **Focus on Empowerment, Not Just "Fixing":**

- *Harnessing Strengths:* Your wisdom can guide others to their own solutions.
- *Navigating Shadows:* Shift your focus from trying to "fix" people or situations to empowering them to find their own strength and solutions. Ask guiding questions rather than giving all the answers. This fosters their agency and reduces your burden.
- *Self-Care:* Remind yourself that everyone is on their own journey, and your role is often to be a compassionate guide or catalyst, not the sole driver of their healing or success.

4. **Discern When to Engage and When to Step Back:**

- *Harnessing Strengths & Navigating Shadows:* Use your deep intuition not only to understand others but also to assess your own energetic capacity and the true potential for positive impact in a situation. It's okay to discern that some situations are not yours to transform, or that your energy is better invested elsewhere.
- *Decision-Making:* Before diving deep into a helping or healing role, ask yourself: "Is this mine

to do? Do I have the capacity? What is the most empowering way I can contribute without depleting myself?" Trust the answers that arise.

The Alchemist Maverick & The Renaissance Themes

Your alchemical nature brings a unique depth to the core Renaissance themes:

- **Redefining Success:** For you, success is often about profound inner growth (yours and others'), healing, making a meaningful difference, and living a life aligned with deep purpose and soul-level truth. It's about the quality of transformation, not just the quantity of achievements.
- **Facing Fear:** Your fears might be subtle, relating to the depth of pain in the world, the fear of not being able to make enough of a difference, or the fear of being overwhelmed by your own empathy. You face these by grounding in your purpose and trusting the transformative process itself.
- **Resilience:** You embody resilience at its deepest level, having learned to not just bounce back from adversity but to transmute it into wisdom, compassion, and strength. Your own journey of alchemy fuels your ability to endure and guide.

- **Taking Risks:** Your risks are often emotional and spiritual, the risk of deep empathy, of entering into broken spaces to facilitate healing, of speaking profound truths that challenge superficiality.
- **Living from Identity:** Your identity is profoundly connected to your capacity for depth, healing, meaning-making, and your role as a soulful guide. Authenticity for you is living in full expression of your compassionate and transformative nature.
- **Building Community:** You build communities of depth, healing, and authentic connection. You create safe spaces where people feel seen in their vulnerability and are supported in their growth and transformation.

Affirmations for the Alchemist Maverick:

- I transform challenges into wisdom and pain into purpose, for myself and others.
- My emotional depth and intuition are powerful guides for healing and growth.
- I honor my own well-being as I support the transformation of others.
- I set compassionate boundaries that protect my energy and sustain my work.
- My presence brings grace, understanding, and a catalyst for positive change.

Journal Prompts for Deeper Reflection:

Reflect on a significant challenge in your life that you transformed into a source of wisdom or purpose. What was the "alchemical" process like for you?

When do you feel most emotionally drained or overextended in your efforts to help others? What's one specific boundary or self-care ritual you can implement this week?

How can you shift from a "fixing" mindset to an "empowering" mindset in a current relationship or situation where you feel called to help?

_____

_____

_____

_____

What does it mean for you to lead with "grace"? How can you bring more of that quality into your interactions and endeavors?

_____

_____

_____

_____

A Renaissance Woman Story: Seraphina, The Peacemaker

Seraphina was a community mediator in a town deeply divided by a contentious local issue. Years of miscommunication and escalating anger had created seemingly irreparable rifts between neighbors, friends, and even families. Many had given up hope for reconciliation.

Seraphina, an Alchemist Maverick, felt called not just to manage the conflict but to facilitate a deeper healing. She knew this wouldn't be easy; the collective pain and mistrust were palpable. Her initial attempts to bring opposing sides together were met with resistance and further outbursts, leaving her feeling the weight of the community's anguish (the Alchemist's shadow of emotional exhaustion).

Instead of pushing harder, Seraphina took a "Maverick Move." She paused the direct mediations and instead initiated a series of small, separate "storytelling circles" with individuals from all sides. She didn't ask them to debate the issue, but simply to share their personal stories, their hopes, and their fears related to the community they all shared. With profound empathy and intuitive questioning, she created a safe space for vulnerability. She listened deeply, absorbing their pain but consciously practicing energetic cleansing each evening to avoid being consumed by it.

Gradually, as people felt truly heard, often for the first time, an alchemical shift began. Seraphina started to gently weave threads of shared values and common humanity from the stories she'd heard, reflecting these back to the groups. When she finally brought larger groups together again, the tone was different. They had glimpsed each other's humanity. While disagreements remained, the vitriol had lessened. Seraphina then guided them through a process of co-creating a "Community Covenant," focusing not on winning or losing, but on how they could live together respectfully despite their differences. It was a long, arduous process, but Seraphina's unwavering belief in their capacity for transformation, her ability to hold space for pain while pointing towards healing, and her commitment to finding meaning even in division helped the town take the first sacred steps toward mending its fractures. She didn't just solve a problem; she helped transform a community's heart.

Embracing Your Sacred Path

Alchemist Maverick, your journey is one of profound depth and purpose. Your ability to navigate the shadows within yourself and in the world, and to emerge with wisdom and grace, is a rare and precious gift. Remember that your own well-being is the sacred vessel from which your transformative work flows. By honoring your energy, setting compassionate boundaries, and focusing on empowering others towards their own alchemy, you can sustain your light and continue to be a beacon of hope, healing, and profound change. Your path is not always easy, but it is undeniably sacred. Walk it with the reverence it deserves.

The Renaissance Is You: A Lifelong Becoming

You've unraveled. You've remembered. You've risen. As you turn these final pages, know that this isn't just the end of a book. It's the beginning of your continued return to self, to purpose, to a power that is uniquely yours. You didn't journey through these chapters merely to be inspired; you came here for something deeper. To reclaim. To redefine. To rise on your own terms. You've explored what it means to stop performing and start embodying, to trade borrowed blueprints for your own authentic design.

In Part I, we walked together through the awakenings necessary to challenge outdated norms and hear the whispers of your own truth. In Part II, by exploring the 7 Renaissance Woman Archetypes, you've hopefully gained a clearer mirror to your innate strengths and a personalized compass for navigating your path forward. You've seen yourself in our stories and, more importantly, in the reflections of the archetypes, not because they dictate your path, but because they echo the multifaceted truth of who you are and the quiet knowing inside you that has always whispered: *There's more than this*. More alignment. More depth. More ownership of your own becoming. More of *you*.

Because your Renaissance doesn't begin, or end, in a spreadsheet, a strategy, or a five-year plan. It unfolds every time you choose: Truth over performance. Integrity over image. Self-trust over outside validation.

We live in a world that often asks women to shrink into roles, into expectations, into polished versions of ourselves that are easier to applaud but harder to sustain. But not you. Not anymore.

You are not here to audition for a life someone else approved. You are not here to chase validation that disappears the moment you rest. You are not here to lead like everyone else. You're here to rewrite the rules entirely. To become the author, the artist, and the architect of your own life. To lead in a way that doesn't just move others, but honors *you*.

And here's what we know for sure: The most powerful transformations don't happen when you force yourself into someone else's blueprint. They happen when you finally say: *I'm ready to lead like me.*

You are not too late. You are not too much. You are right on time and right on purpose. This is your permission to expand. To disrupt. To soften. To rise louder. Or quieter.

To lead boldly. Or rest deeply. To take up space without apology and without explanation. Because that's what a Renaissance Woman does, she returns to herself. Over and over again. And with every return, she rises differently. More rooted. More real. More free.

If this book spoke to your spirit, we invite you to go deeper. Our Renaissance Workshops, programs, and community are immersive spaces designed to help women like you stop performing, start aligning, and build bold momentum, together. These aren't just events or courses; they are catalysts, mirrors, and the potential next chapter of your becoming. You've read our stories and explored the archetypes. Now it's time to continue writing your own

This isn't goodbye. This is your next beginning. This is your homecoming. This is your continuous return to power.

The Renaissance is you.

AUTHORS BIOS

About Melissa Aarskaug

 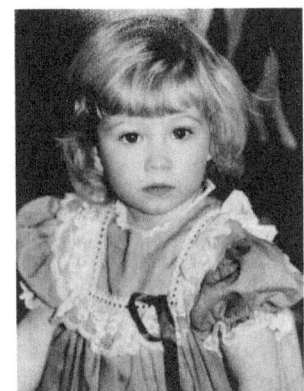

(Melissa at 2)

A true modern Renaissance Woman, Melissa Aarskaug has built a career at the intersection of reinvention, leadership, and impact. With a trajectory that spans civil engineering, regulatory compliance, cybersecurity, and executive leadership, she embodies the essence of evolving fearlessly and leading with clarity, compassion, and confidence.

Melissa is a respected executive and strategist, known for guiding organizations through transformation and empowering individuals to lead with intention. Over the course of her career, she has consistently driven meaningful growth both in sales performance and business strategy by aligning teams, building trust, and navigating complexity with calm, focused leadership. Her success spans across highly regulated industries, where her ability to translate vision into results has made her a trusted partner and advisor.

She is also the creator of *Executive Connect,* a multi-dimensional platform that spans podcasting, live events, books, and curated experiences. Centered around the guiding promise to Break Free, Design Your Legacy, *Executive Connect* invites today's and tomorrow's leaders to challenge the status quo, redefine success, and build lives and careers of lasting impact.

Melissa is a sought-after speaker in regulated industries, including casino gaming, cybersecurity, and emerging technologies, where she brings clarity to complexity and inspires new ways of thinking. Her insights have been featured in global publications including *Success Magazine*, *Indian Gaming Magazine*, *Gaming and Leisure Magazine*, and *Global Gaming Business (GGB)*. She has also received honors such as the Patricia Becker Pay It Forward Award and Emerging Leaders of Gaming 40 Under 40.

Whether she's writing, speaking, or leading strategy sessions, Melissa brings a distinct ability to bridge big vision with practical action. She's passionate about helping others turn struggle into strength, using her own journey of reinvention as a blueprint for transformation. Through *Executive Connect* and beyond, Melissa champions a new model of leadership, one rooted in resilience, reinvention, and authenticity. Her mission is to help others unlock what's possible when they choose to live boldly, lead intentionally, and design their legacy on their own terms.

aarskaugm@gmail.com
https://www.executiveconnectexperience.com/
https://www.linkedin.com/in/melissa-aarskaug/
https://www.instagram.com/melissa_aarskaug/
https://x.com/melissaaarskaug/
https://www.tiktok.com/@melissa_aarskaug

About Michele Kline

(Michele at 4)

With a journey rooted in reinvention and fierce intentionality, Argentinean immigrant Michele Kline has made a career out of shaking things up—for the better. A fixer of broken processes, connector of humans, and coach with a heart, Michele blends process mastery with people magic to spark real, lasting change.

Since founding Kline Hospitality Consulting in 2010, she's worked across the boardroom and the breakroom, coaching leaders and transforming teams in global hospitality giants, gaming and entertainment empires, tech titans, and Fortune 500 companies. Her mission? Turn chaos into clarity, burnout into boldness, and meetings into movement.

Michele's approach ditches stale training manuals in favor of engaging, just-in-time coaching and dynamic, hands-on workshops that actually stick. Whether she's helping executives level up their communication and leadership style, guiding high-potential leaders through mindset breakthroughs, or coaching the next generation of minds ages 11–17, Michele brings her signature blend of neuroscience-based tools, continuous improvement strategies, and no-fluff conversations to every room she walks into.

With an academic background in communication and certifications in Coaching, Kaizen, Total Quality Management, Six Sigma, Human Resources, and Neuroscience-based methodologies, Michele is as sharp as she is soulful. Her superpower? Helping leaders rewire their brains, build stronger habits, and lead with guts, grace, and a whole lot of heart.

 An eight-time international bestselling author, Michele's latest book, *360° IMPACT: A Guide to Live, Lead, and Serve in a More Colorful World!*, shot to #1 across multiple categories and countries. She also co-authored all six powerhouse volumes of the *Becoming an Unstoppable Woman* series—each hitting #1 Amazon Bestseller status in categories ranging from entrepreneurship to health across the globe.

Off the page, Michele is an award-winning coach, keynote speaker, and co-host of the unapologetically real leadership podcast *WTF! Walk The Floors*, where she reminds listeners that leadership isn't about titles—it's about action. Roll up your sleeves. Walk the floors. Own the impact.

With *Renaissance*, Michele continues her mission to help modern Mavericks redefine success, ditch the rules that never fit, and create lives and careers that feel as good as they look. Her message is clear: Lead loud. Live fully. Color outside the lines—and never shrink to fit.

www.klinehospitality.com
info@klinehospitality.com
https://www.linkedin.com/in/michelekline/
https://www.instagram.com/micheleklinekhc/

RENAISSANCE STORY

Melissa and Michele met over 16 years ago, and from the moment their paths crossed, it was as though they had known each other forever. Kindred spirits in every sense of the term, they quickly became soulmates in thought, action, and ambition. Despite their uncanny similarities, their journeys to success couldn't have been more different. Melissa's path was paved with leaps of faith and bold reinvention, while Michele's was a testament to resilience, community building, and steady growth. Yet, through all their triumphs and trials, they discovered that their core values were the same—values that now serve as the foundation of their brand, *Renaissance*.

The Renaissance Philosophy

At the heart of *Renaissance* lies a simple yet profound belief: You can have it all. Success doesn't have to come at the cost of happiness, family, or personal fulfillment. Melissa and Michele built this brand to empower others to push the reset button, redefine where they stand today, and chart a course toward a brighter, more balanced future.

Both women know what it means to face fear, take risks, and grow through discomfort. They understand the power of community, the strength found in resilience, and the joy of breaking through barriers that once seemed insurmountable – shared lessons drawn from the very soul of *Renaissance*.

The Renaissance Mission

Together, Melissa and Michele founded *Renaissance* to guide others through the process of redefining their lives. Their brand isn't about chasing someone else's version of success; it's about creating your own.

Renaissance offers tools, stories, and actionable strategies to help people break free from limits and design lives they truly love.

An Invitation to Transform

Melissa and Michele believe that everyone has the power to rewrite their story. Whether it's finding courage to take that first step, rebuilding after a setback, or connecting with others to build something greater than oneself, *Renaissance* is a rallying cry for transformation. It's more than a brand; it's a movement—a reminder that no matter where you are in life, it's never too late to rise, reinvent, and thrive.

With Renaissance, readers are invited to step into a life of possibility and purpose; to prove that you can push past fear, embrace change, and discover what it truly means to have it all.

Keynotes

Melissa and Michele bring their energy, wisdom, and authenticity to the stage through dynamic keynote speeches. These talks are tailored to inspire and challenge audiences to rethink their approaches to success, growth, and resilience. Whether it's a corporate event, leadership summit, or community gathering, their messages resonate deeply and leave a lasting impact.

Workshops

The *Renaissance* workshops dive deep into the principles of growth, resilience, and reinvention. Participants engage in hands-on exercises, reflective activities, and collaborative discussions designed to spark transformation. This immersive experience provides practical tools and strategies for personal and professional breakthroughs.

Retreats

Melissa and Michele's retreats offer a holistic approach to transformation. Set in serene, inspiring locations, these multi-day experiences combine introspection, connection, and action. Attendees are guided through activities that help them reconnect with their purpose, overcome fears, and create a vision for the life they want to lead. The retreats foster a sense of community and provide a safe space for deep personal growth.

Coaching

To keep the momentum going and build a community of like-minded individuals, Michele offers coaching sessions. These sessions create a space for ongoing growth, accountability, and support. Participants engage in discussions, share progress, and receive guidance to stay on track with their goals while connecting with others on similar journeys. The group coaching experience reinforces the sense of belonging and collective empowerment that lies at the heart of *Renaissance*.

INK YOUR INSIGHTS HERE

accomplished:
- I've retired from client work to build the next ten years
- fix dinner / experiment

leaving behind
a ~~this need to~~
engagement w/
anyone w/ bad
vibes

reinvest: redefine:

18584649R00136